Dr Wendy Jordan Thomson is an English author living in Jersey. A farmer's daughter, turned clinician, who has tried to make a difference in whatever capacity she found herself: as a therapist, scientific researcher, writer, farmer and inventor. She draws on her clinical experience while also working on research at the Medical Research Unit at Graylingwell Psychiatric Hospital in Sussex.

Dedicated to the vulnerable and those who love them enough to make a difference.

Dr Wendy Jordan Thomson

UNPACKING TODAY'S TURMOIL

Know Thyself

AUSTIN MACAULEY PUBLISHERS™

LONDON · CAMBRIDGE · NEW YORK · SHARJAH

A CIP catalogue record for this title is available from the British Library.

ISBN 9781528977692 (Paperback)
ISBN 9781528977715 (ePub e-book)

www.austinmacauley.com

First Published (2020)
Austin Macauley Publishers Ltd
25 Canada Square
Canary Wharf
London
E14 5LQ

My thanks to all the patients I was most privileged to meet and whose resilience I respect. To my husband, Ian, who was such a willing sounding board. To Esther in the USA and the readership internationally, who by painstakingly downloading my case studies and research, prompted this book. And finally to the publishers who believed in the need for this book.

Prologue

This book is neither intended to be a clinical textbook nor is it intended to be controversial or written from any one school of thought. Within the book is an account of what I found and how I developed a treatment technique to suit the needs of my patients: a common-sense, bottom-up, practical approach to help patients deal with their behaviour, feelings and predicaments, the majority of which are the consequences of living in a fast-changing, insecure world and the complexity of the mind.

However, I do believe it is a long-overdue book, written from the standpoint of the children and adult patients whom I treated and who became victims through reacting to circumstances, over which they had little or no control, or decisions they made without the education, wisdom or the information and maturity needed to cope with often-overwhelming difficulties. I have also tried to give a portrayal of how they have needed to fit into a system which is not best suited to them. This was typified by them asking the question (only when they trusted me) "Am I going mad?" – just because they had been referred to a psychiatric service.

This is further typified from the point of view of the general public when discussing the local asylum: "The only thing right about that place is the clock." An omniscient reminder which struck the hour in the cathedral town. For mental illness is still feared and still possesses the aura of being bewitched, the esoteric, the no-go area, revealing how little we know about and understand ourselves.

This book is also written in response to the professionals who have read my research and articles and who appear to enjoy and use the case studies to teach and educate their students. And for those who have laboriously downloaded my publications, I have been motivated to gather everything together in one volume. So, in summary, this is a book for everyone, including patients who can identify with those included in the case studies.

However, it reflects a gloomy picture: statistics from the World Health Organisation (WHO) from October 2018, consider that one in four people in the world will be affected by mental or neurological disorders at some point in their lives. Around 450 million people currently suffer from such conditions, placing mental disorders among the leading causes of ill-health and disability worldwide.

WHO's Mental Health Action Plan 2013–2020, endorsed by the World Health Assembly in 2013, recognises the essential role of mental health in achieving health for all people. The plan includes four major objectives:

1. Provide more effective leadership and governance for mental health;
2. Provide comprehensive, integrated mental health and social care services in community-based settings;
3. Implement strategies for promotion and prevention and
4. Strengthen information systems, evidence and research. (But what is missing are the means by which implementation takes place and enforcement. It sounds an alarmingly bureaucratic directive to me and lacks zeal. Also missing from these objectives is the psychosomatic link between physical and mental illness as my research has found and emphasised. So, I'm bound to ask where the teeth are!)

My various published case studies have been intended to help those caring for patients experiencing psychic pain and to present the outcome if the patients don't get the support they need.

There is no excuse. For years, for example, the suicide rate has increased. Theory and statistical trends are businesses in themselves, but what is their value if nobody does anything? Data is dead unless activated.

An estimated one million people worldwide die by suicide every year. It is estimated that global annual suicide fatalities could rise to over 1.5 million by 2020. Globally, suicide ranks among the three leading causes of death among those aged 15–44 years. Attempted suicides are up to 20 times more frequent than completed ones.

Stories told from patients' perspectives indicate that they need personal strategies aimed at prevention via families who are committed to their welfare and schools with curriculums equipping them for life to help them make the right decisions, to warn them when there's danger and to show them how to avoid problems. They need a defence against a turbulent society.

This book is an attempt to make the point that but for the grace of God, we too could become a vulnerable, mentally ill patient. I hope this book lays bare the facts in such an honest and factual manner that the conclusion drawn from it reinforces the standpoint that every case is understandable. And if we too were to find ourselves in such circumstances, we too would join the multitudes of people who just cannot cope with the intolerable life circumstances they find themselves in.

I am not following my colleagues who suggest more resources and money should be thrown at prevention and intervention by way of treatment. The problems highlighted require a different, more common-sense and pragmatic way of seeing things, things in society which need remedying such as marrying for infatuation, having children without the necessary commitment to their overall well-being, failing to equip children with the foundation they need to thrive and succeed, and schools educating children for a large part of their developmental lives. However, I can't help wondering if education isn't failing to teach about the core needs of every child – survival.

For those who do need treatment, therapists need to understand psychopathology from the point of view of the patient. They need to use the suffering which can be tapped to harness their creativity, making their experiences part of the journey, turning them around. However bad a child's background, if they have survived so far, it speaks volumes about their self-belief and their resilience, and that resilience can be a key factor in their future. It can become the fuel to drive them forward. They then can become good parents and good citizens rather than being a burden on society.

Professionals involved in treating and caring frequently come from very different backgrounds, so often far removed from those of their patients. The professionals are often privileged and have enjoyed feelings of love and security. They have no idea, despite their best endeavours, of how to empathise with or comprehend what it is like to be a child whose parents feed them drugs to keep them quiet while they go out partying or to be forced to have sex because their parents are exploiting them. Such cases are often never disclosed, because the victims from experience know full well that they will never be understood or believed. Extreme victims of incest or paedophilia, for example, have experienced things so abhorrent they can never be fully healed, so compromises have to be made and understood. The task is enormous. The point I am making is that these vulnerable patients are very wary. They test out where and to whom and if it is safe to disclose these past experiences. It was not unusual for me to see patients who had been receiving treatment all their lives but had never felt enough trust to divulge their experiences. Therapists often lack the same power generated by adversity; they need to taste pain and acknowledge what is missing from their toolkit.

When I was new to psychiatry, having come from a background of physical therapy and rehabilitation, I was perplexed by the diagnostic criteria used in psychiatry: neurosis, depression, schizophrenia, personality disorders, etc. I felt inferior because I did not understand the nature and causes of those various illnesses. One of the first elements of this confusion for me was the openness with which my former patients discussed their physical illness, such as trauma and fractures, neurological illnesses, strokes and disseminated sclerosis. Those patients with physical illness, in some cases, used their illnesses as trophies; for example, a biker, who had sustained multiple fractures, nearly losing his life from 'doing a ton' down Watford bypass, swanked that he could not wait to get back onto his bike and pick up from where he'd left off? This was ignoring the huge cost of receiving hospital treatment for over a year, and a great deal of care and commitment from a large number of staff, not to mention the worry suffered by his family over a prolonged period.

However, patients with mental illness were ashamed. The psychiatric patients felt the whole weight of being dubbed a psychiatric patient. The physically ill were visited with flowers, fruit and cards. Not so the psychiatric patients; their visitors did not want to be seen near the hospital as if they could become infected in some way. The stigma of becoming a psychiatric case was in itself another difficulty, an additional burden which further confounded attempts towards treatment and resolution, irrespective of the diagnosis. Agreeing to be referred to the psychiatric service was, for some, a stamp of inferiority which remained with the patient throughout their recovery and beyond. It was tantamount to throwing in the towel. Not the best start for me as a therapist needing to motivate them and mobilise a belief in themselves. As Jung stated, the diagnosis is for the benefit of the clinician, not for the benefit of the patient.

This denial borne out of fear, confusion and ignorance on the one hand, with its associated stigma of being a psychiatric patient, compared with the wholehearted acceptance of a physical illness on the other hand, was a problem I began to understand, not only on a personal level for the patient, but also acknowledging that a psychiatric diagnosis affected the referring doctor's relationship with his/her patient, with the patient's family, work place and friends. Sensitive general practitioners (GPs) realised full well that suggesting that their patient needed psychiatric help had, in some cases, severe consequences. It became very clear that the psychiatric service was used by certain GPs, whereas some chose never to refer. It was, therefore, no surprise to me that when I worked in a confidential drop-in centre, it was not only used, but it very quickly needed to expand to cope with the demand. This was a confidential service whereby the patient was in control. This is discussed in several of the chapters below.

My scientific research answered hypotheses which I had constructed, but the gap between the patients and the research perspective was extensive. I could understand this confusion because I too had the same experience. My first research attempted to address the relationship between the physical and the psychological, the psyche versus soma. Looking back, I can now realise that this research, although part of a dissertation, was in reality much more personal; it was my attempt to bridge the gap between the physical and the mental, and in effect, confirm that they are inextricably linked.

There is, in my opinion, no argument for seeing the patient from just a psychological or a physical point of view. They should be seen as a co-evolving system – a whole. This system needs to include all relationships, whether physical, psychological, social or educational. The personal identity, including the genealogical and biological background – all becomes part of a patient's life and journey and is, therefore, relevant. This concept embracing everything needs to be understood and unpacked jointly by the patient and the therapist/professional in a collaborative manner. What I am advocating will, no doubt, cause some to say that we haven't got time to engage in this manner and in this depth with patients. My defence would be that it doesn't take a lot of time because the patients improve rapidly and, in the long run, they can be discharged, better equipped for the future than previously. The therapist is kick-starting a journey which engages the creativeness of the patients, which can be very exciting. They don't become chronic dysfunctional members of society, making more and more demands and always bearing a grudge and making no contribution to society. They can become vibrant people with more control and more optimism.

The journey of our lives may appear totally random. It may feel we have been dealt a good or a bad hand. Patients need to understand their journey, and having dealt with the past, look to the future renewed and adjusted. There is nearly always a need for patients to understand the how, the why, and what will happen as a result of their illness and their particular diagnosis. Our prime task as parents, professionals, therapists and teachers is to understand the journey. There may need to be emphasis on either the past, the present or particular elements, but these definitely need to include the future. So, as the journey becomes complex, untangling causative factors, nothing can be excluded when ticking all boxes, which amount to the unique person we have come to be within the here and now. I have always sold this unpacking as an exciting journey as 'perhaps the most exciting journey you will ever take'. This is a far cry from taking a pill, not knowing what it is for and the effect it might have.

In writing this book, I also need to explain that as well as being a researcher, I have served as a physical therapist, a family therapist and then a general psychotherapist. Thus, I will do my best to indicate when and how I fused these different working criteria. Each influence has been important, and as my training increased, I was able to incorporate various aspects within my existing knowledge. But beyond a shadow of a doubt, my greatest legacy came from the patients and their families trusting me, telling me their innermost fears, telling me their stories and their narratives, allowing me to get onto their wavelengths. I was merely the conductor, blending in the parts, bringing together the various elements and fusing them towards the harmony and the climax in one performance.

However, it has also been a confusing journey for me, trying to get onto the wavelength of my colleagues whose training has been different and with whom I worked in various settings. Each time I changed jobs, there was a different emphasis, for example, from physical rehabilitation to treating brain-damaged children, to psychiatry, family therapy, psychotherapy and management, and I had to adjust. The thread that has connected these various beginnings and departures has been my research.

Although this book has focused on family dynamics and treatment, my main concern for the future is with prevention, and how to prevent the reactions of living in today's turmoil.

Chapter 1
History of Psychiatry and Family Therapy

Psychiatry

This first chapter provides a brief historical background concerning general psychiatry. This is then followed briefly by a snapshot of the history of family therapy. Psychiatry has a chequered history, which is helpfully summarised by Neel Burton, the author of *The Meaning of Madness*:

Psychiatry, like most medical specialties, has a continuing, significant need for research into its diseases, classifications and treatments. Psychiatry has adopted from biology the fundamental belief that disease and health are different elements of an individual's adaptation to an environment. But psychiatry also recognises that the environment of the human species is complex and includes physical, cultural and interpersonal elements. In addition to external factors, the human brain must contain and organise an individual's hopes, fears, desires, fantasies and feelings. Psychiatry's difficult task is to bridge the understanding of these factors so that they can be studied both clinically and physiologically.

In the latter part of the twentieth century, neuroimaging techniques, genetic studies and pharmacological breakthroughs such as the first antipsychotic drug, chlorpromazine, completely reversed this psychoanalytical model of mental disorder and prompted a return to a more biological, 'neo-Kraepelinian' model. At present, mental disorders are primarily seen as a biological disorder of the brain, although it is also recognised that psychological and social stressors can play important roles in triggering episodes of illness and that different approaches to treatment should be seen not as competing but as complementary.

However, critics tend to deride this 'bio-psycho-social' model as little more than a 'bio-bio-bio' model, with psychiatrists reduced to mere diagnosticians and pill-pushers. Many critics question the scientific evidence underpinning such a robust biological approach and call for a radical rethink of mental disorders, not as detached disease processes that can be apportioned diagnostic labels, but as subjective and meaningful experiences grounded in both personal and larger sociocultural narratives.

Psychiatry, as this testimony suggests, is not cut and dry. I maintain that all the children, and a high proportion of the adults, were reacting to situational conditions and needed to understand why they had succumbed to extreme psychosocial pressures.

Family Therapy

Informal intervention within families is not new; throughout history, various people have played a role in family crises, such as priests, doctors, friends, relatives, tribal chiefs and witch-doctors. In Africa, for example, if a family member is brought by the family to the doctor, the doctor will ask, "Who is responsible for this person?" The tribe will know who is responsible and can identify that person. Similarly, if the tribe wants help for that person, the whole extended family will crowd in to attend the consultation. In 1989, I witnessed this at first hand in Africa; a man was brought manacled into a hut (which served as the consulting room). His whole family was there to see what the psychiatrist would recommend. The psychiatrist said that the man needed to have an antipsychotic injection, and for that, he must be set free from the manacles and escorted to the nurse. As a result, once the manacles were removed, the patient made a run for it. He was rugby-tackled by the family and was taken to the nurse to have the injection.

Formal family therapy as a profession probably had its origins in the social work movement of nineteenth-century United Kingdom, following John Bowlby at the Tavistock Clinic in London and his work on attachment theory. Most of the early founders of the field of family therapy had a psychoanalytic background. In the 1950s, the general systems theory, which focused on the role of communication, was introduced into psychology and psychotherapy. In the mid-60s, distinct schools of family therapy emerged which emphasised subjective experience and unexpressed feelings, including the unconscious.

From the mid-1980s up until the present day, family therapy has followed various approaches that partly reflect the original schools. These schools include brief therapy, structural therapy and constructivist approaches.

Family therapy is the branch of psychotherapy that views the family as a system, whereby any interaction by one member of the family has a contingent reaction on the rest of the family. The family therapist works with the family to achieve change and adjustment, which aims to restore order and health.

According to Booth (2000), there is still a significant number of therapists who adhere more or less strictly to a particular approach which appeals to them personally. Lebow (2005) believed that many practitioners claimed to be eclectic, using techniques from several areas depending upon their own inclinations and/or the needs of the clients. There is a growing movement towards a single, generic form of family therapy that seeks to incorporate the best of the accumulated knowledge in the field and which can be adapted to many different contexts.

Chapter 2
What Method?

"What method do you employ?" was one of the responses that I received, following the publication of one of my case studies. This was the first reason that prompted me to write this book. The second reason was because of the interest generated by the case studies that have been published. The editor told me that the studies 'increased the readership of the journal'. The fact is that I neither knew what method I used nor did I know how unique my experience as a family therapist was. Having retrospectively studied the various schools, I would describe my training as very much based on Jungian psychology, but my own approach has been very eclectic and personally formulated.

Perhaps a little background information is pertinent here.

I think it is salient that I did not select family therapy; rather, it chose me (I have more to say about selection, but I will leave it for later in the book). I had just finished a post-graduate university course in rehabilitation, management and research, and was in between jobs and considering my options. One day, I was getting into my car to go shopping, stepping around the sheep that had gathered outside the farmhouse where I lived sheltered by the downs, when a child psychiatrist arrived in his car. I had only met him once when I attended a psychotherapy training group that he had been running. I didn't know him very well. He had come to ask whether I would consider becoming a psychotherapist because he had an opening on his staff. I was rather flattered, but I told him that I did not think that this was the right direction for me to go. I told him my interest was in research. He became quite persuasive and suggested that I apply and see what happened – after all, I had nothing to lose.

Well, I agreed that I had nothing to lose. After many exhaustive interviews, I was offered the job, and I decided to take it despite the fact that I did not consider myself a psychotherapist.

The family therapy unit consisted of the child psychiatrist, a secretary and three family therapists. In lieu of a commitment to lecturing and training social workers and GPs, the child psychiatrist would have a number of trainees attending the family therapy unit for supervision within the unit. These trainees would take on cases that they managed while under his supervision. In practice, the unit was assumed to overlap with the adult psychiatric service. The training was in-house, and it worked like this: referrals to the family therapy unit were made by GPs, educational welfare officers and social services social workers.

Supervision took the form of attending a ward round at the children's hospital, going to various lectures and attending the supervision sessions. The idea was that during the supervision sessions, therapists shared their cases and learned by discussing the cases presented in the presence of the psychiatrist. Each therapist was also assessed by the letters that they needed to send to the various referral sources. Looking back, I think that the psychiatrist, who happened to be Jungian, adopted a sink or swim strategy; he felt that each therapist had to develop his/her own strategies to cope with families. Those who couldn't cope and did not possess the necessary resilience left. And a considerable number did leave.

It was a tough beginning and very worrying; the supervision sessions were often humiliating and uncomfortable – so uncomfortable that trainees would try to avoid them. They would make up excuses for not attending or for being late. No one wanted to expose themselves and then be criticised in front of their peers. However, if they avoided these difficult sessions, then it implied that they had no problems in managing their particular caseload. So, was it at their peril that they missed them?

The letters we had to write to the referral source were another source of worry; if the letter failed to succinctly and accurately lay out the formulation, separating the form and content and offering a diagnosis and plan for each case, they were unceremoniously torn up. Occasionally, the letters had to be redrafted many times. The psychiatrist believed that the family therapy unit should educate, and the letters were the means by which the referral source was informed of their patients' progress or potential pitfalls. More seriously, the letters revealed inappropriate formulations and weaknesses on the part of the therapists and exposed their failings.

Then, there were the families with a multitude of difficulties that varied from the serious to the trivial. A request for a bell and pad for a child suffering from enuresis might appear, at first, to be trivial. However, it could turn out to be the reactive symptoms of destructive undercurrents threatening the child's future development and perhaps something even more sinister. It was a very serious business, which depended on the ability of the therapist to engage with the family, using awareness to dig and delve below the surface. It was all too easy to issue a bell and pad and write a letter of discharge; no one would be any the wiser.

For those who may be unaware, the bell and pad was an electrical device placed in the bed to stop enuresis. Directly moisture made contact with the pad, it triggered a series of alarms, allowing parents to jump out of bed and escort the child to the toilet before the bed became really wet. The bell became progressively louder, so there was an incentive to race to the bed before the bell awoke the whole family. Stories abounded following the issue of those enuresis deterrents. For example, a child who directly triggered the bell would, in an awakened stupor, leave his bed and disappear down a corridor to mistakenly water flower pots, etc. Or parents, both responding to the bell by jumping out of bed, would collide with the other in the bedroom door to get to the child. And then, having tucked up the child back into his bed, the parents needed to relieve themselves before resuming their disturbed night's sleep. The idea against issuing anyone the bell and pad was that it needed to be determined whether the child was just a heavy sleeper or if the enuresis was a symptom of an emotional disorder, as in the case of Veronica (discussed below).

I benefitted from this 'baptism by fire' approach in the family therapy unit. Although I too, was initially tempted to avoid the supervision sessions, but I then realised that if I braved presenting a worrying case, I didn't have to hide my mistakes – after all, I was learning from them. So, I progressed to actually enjoying the supervision, daring to be spontaneous while risking criticism. I realised that the more discomfort I experienced during supervision, the sharper and the more resilient I became in my role as a family therapist.

As therapists, we had no resources other than ourselves. There were no hospital beds or prescription pads and being tough and resilient went with the territory. Our toolkit was our intuition, awareness, imagination, observation, knowledge, experience and empathy. We also had to take risks, when necessary, to decide when to confront. To embrace and enjoy the diverse challenges alone, with no one to hold our hands was frightening in the beginning; however, it was also exhilarating. When children's lives are at stake, the intervention must be effective. The only supportive links we had were the supervision sessions. But they were tenuous; no one knew the whole picture except for the therapist. Supervision was reliant on the portrayal of the facts; however, if those facts were massaged or misrepresented, whether consciously or unconsciously, then no one could see the whole picture and give advice.

Initially, it was daunting to arrange a meeting in the home of a family, to view the problems within the family and to feel the weight of the responsibility. Quite often, we were unwelcome. And then there was composing the letter to the referral source, explaining the family dynamics and formulating a plan for dealing with the problem. I developed a personal method: I would read the referral, make an appointment to see the family all together and observe the dynamics and what was said in the first instance. Then I would leave to work at the problem, identifying salient points, the main players and the victims. I might return to corroborate my initial hunch. Then, once I was certain, I'd make a plan and I could relax. The psychiatrist once asked me if I trusted my intuition. I replied that I did to a point. He said, "Trust it. You will be right." The result was that, as if to confirm I was on the right track, the children, who were all merely reacting to the family dynamics, would improve. Unlike other therapists who never discharged their patients because they never could, I would be able to discharge relatively quickly. My main concern was always to devote enough thought to each case early on; then, from there it was maintenance, liaison and downhill. I was my own check and balancer. I liked setting up a mini-challenge for myself: how long to crack the core case, then augment with psychotherapy, practical input, discharge? So exciting!

Chapter 3
Blood on Our Hands

We have created a vicious, co-evolving circle of disorder – a societal, political and economic consumer-driven society, epitomised by divorce instability and by children whose role models are either rock stars or footballers. This unstable and unsustainable society robs children of their foundational needs to develop and thrive, emotionally and physically. They become disorientated and insecure, lack trust and have no self-identity. They then self-treat with mind-altering substances such as alcohol and drugs.

Recently, Colin, a car technician in Jersey, told me how extensive drug use is. He related to me that if he goes to instruct away from home where hospitality is the order of the day, he's offered cocaine on a regular basis. He told me that the younger generation of apprentices take this as a normal adjunct to a night out. Some will use these drugs recreationally, but to those who are insecure, depressed and miserable, it will only need one pill to lift their mood to get hooked, so much so that it will quickly become addictive and habitual. Of course, the pushers are well aware of this vulnerability and exploit it to increase their business.

Naturally, prevention is the real need, but being realistic, it would need the equivalence of a cultural tsunami to re-set the sociological clock and prevent the causal disorder within existing global societies. Provision is woefully inadequate in terms of rehabilitation, particularly when no attention is given to the personal stories of these patients. Therapy, particularly medication, cannot undo these foundational deficiencies. Using the example of one of my patients, any attempt towards intervention or therapy does, at the very least, need to empathise with those patients, and on a one-to-one basis, get onto their wavelength and understand their stories, their narratives. I cannot imagine what that patient would feel like if offered a tablet to remedy his psychic pain after re-living and disclosing his story.

Forgive me if I digress and use Alexander Fleming to make the point. If you recall, he was the scientist who discovered penicillin when he worked in a laboratory in Saint Mary's hospital in Paddington London. My connection with him was via his colleague. They were both Scottish and friends. I was working with his wife who was herself, a distinguished researcher and practitioner in tropical and community medicine. She suggested I meet with her husband in their home to discuss the treatment provision for drug abuse. I remember the idyllic setting their home set beneath downs, where from the window, I could see sheep grazing contentedly outside. But nothing could have prepared me for what happened next inside. On the small coffee table, there was a book, and as we sipped tea, I was told that the friend of Alexander Fleming was reading the autobiography of Alexander Fleming. At that very time, I was coincidently also reading the biography of Alexander Fleming. This was even more of a coincidence because at the time, I never read due to my commitments to family and work which meant that there was never time. To my amazement and delight, he then fetched the phial containing the original penicillin? It was to put it mildly incredulous! But returning to the really central point, Fleming was humble enough to acknowledge that if he had read the Bible, he would have found the foundational antibiotic years before and would have saved the lives of many dying from infections during and following the war. His humility, together with his complete dedication to heal the sick, was exemplary. Unlike so many nowadays who exploit their ideas, Fleming never tried to sell his discovery, seeing it as a contribution towards the greater good of humanity.

As a scientist and therapist, and assuming no comparison to the achievements of Alexander Fleming, I do understand the need for both the objectivity of scientific endeavour and the subjectivity involved with dealing with individuals. I also emphasise the importance of the two, needing to work in tandem: practical common sense and the verifiable scientific method, something which the humble Fleming, realised and acknowledged in the book. Which brings me to the point I am making: solving and unravelling problems scientifically can confound and undermine the solutions which might need to be based just on common sense. The simplest strategies in most walks of life is prevention: to have the knowledge and wisdom to live within the confines and boundaries in which life is equitable and not to court danger and provoke illness and disorder in the wider context.

To enable this preventative strategy to work, the individual needs to be equipped for the purpose of living a contented, manageable, disciplined life. Family, school and society provide the foundational basis for becoming wise and mature adults, enabling members to live contentedly and prosper, and then to nurture their own children in a similar manner. However, in this respect, my feeling is that children have been, and what is more, still are being failed. It doesn't need science to verify how they are failing. It is, sadly, all too evident.

When I was working in the realm of family therapy and psychiatry, I realised how crucial part the narrative played in therapy. Not only did the therapist need to understand the past of patients and how they had come to need help, but also the patients needed to better understand themselves. Then, together we would work to untangle where things had gone wrong, enabling us to move forward. I would give them homework, and one of the assignments was to write their journey so far. Some were barely literate because they had missed schooling, such as William, whose case study is presented below. I'd learn so much from their writing autobiographical accounts of their lives. It would augment the one-to-one sessions I had with them. Rereading them now, some years later, I am moved by the stories they told.

One such story is of Jake (he cannot write in lower case; he prints by hand all in upper case). Jake relates how, at the age of eight, his father started to physically abuse him. His father used to send him, but not his sister, to bed at six o'clock. He couldn't understand why. His mother was loving and would stick up for Jake, which in turn, his father resented. His father eventually left home and divorced his mother, who then remarried. Jake was nine at the time. This second marriage 'wasn't happy'. His stepfather was silent and never talked. Jake's mother then became ill with kidney trouble, and Jake would come home from school to find her crying, doubled up in pain. He described her as shivering and sweating. But seeing him upset, she would take him in her arms and say, "We must be brave." She was eventually forced to go into hospital.

One day, Jake came home from school to find relatives he had never seen before in the house. He was sent to his bedroom, wondering what was happening and, after a long time, the news was broken to him that his mother had died. Jake was then told that, the next day, he had to go to live with his biological father and his new wife. This stepmother hated Jake from the start, and when he came home from school, she told him to stay away. Even if it was raining and cold, he could not go into the house. Jake mentions how he found a little girl friend and thought his father would be pleased to meet her, but instead, his father hit Jake and pushed the girl towards the door. Jake shouted to the girl, "Get out!" and she fled. His father then told Jake to get out. Jake was put in a home. He says that, in some ways, he was glad but, in his words, "I felt very lonely, and friends and school didn't matter anymore." From then on, he went from one institution to another, ending up in a penitentiary and prison. This is what he writes: *Why? Well, that's easily answered, because I was very lonely and bored with every job I ever had. I felt unwanted by everything and everybody. I just lacked the guts of a human being to stand up and fight my way to my destiny. I didn't trust myself or anybody so what chance did I have?*

Reading Jake's story makes me feel ashamed that, with all our scientific progress and achievements, we cannot responsibly care for children such as Jake. As a therapist, I know Jake would never emotionally catch up: his schooling was jeopardised, and this would prevent him from reaching and maintaining a fulfilling career and a contented life. His mistrust was foundational instead of the trust which every child needs to feel secure and develop. I've experienced these children 'testing me out'. It's their means of getting the assurance they need to trust. This mechanism is, of course, counterproductive because not every potential helper/therapist can withstand this provocation.

But I would like to pick up on three words from Jake's story that jump off the page for me: Guts, fight and trust. However, I would reverse them. First, Jake needed the trust, and then the resilience and belief in himself to, as he says, fight. Quite naturally, he shouldn't have to fight, but this is precisely the situation children find themselves in. They see themselves as needing to fight society. What a terrible society that must seem to them! It goes without saying that the foundation of love and security necessary for every child should be their birth-right. We don't need science to verify that. But sadly, with the disruptive turmoil surrounding divorce, the lack of stability in family life, together with the corrupting influence provided by the media, children such as Jake are like chaff blowing in the wind, lacking roots, a sense of identity and personal worth. They so often feel guilty and responsible for situations over which they have no control. Jake, aged nine, felt tormented by his mother's illness but guilty because he could do nothing about it, only be brave as his mother had instructed him. He was tormented by not being able to prevent his mother's death.

I must admit that when family planning was made possible through contraception, I thought there would be fewer unwanted pregnancies, thus sparing children from the loneliness and desperateness of being left or unwanted. But I was wrong. The sanctity of the family has been further dissipated, with a loss of the foundational requirements for a child to develop.

My research has supported the hypotheses that premature death is a consequence of a depressive illness (Thomson, 1986, 2011, 2012, 2014, 2016, 2017) and that stress is correlated with personality (Thomson, 1980, 1986). But as important as these findings are towards our understanding of psychopathology, they do nothing to prevent children becoming men like Jake, leading miserable, unfulfilled lives which society can only sustain by providing various hospitals, rehabilitation units, reformatories and, ultimately, penitentiaries and containment.

The research merely provides evidence of the correlations between physical, mental and social well-being, which is all common sense. But if, together, they can only present causal correlational relationships and no progress is made at prevention, then, in my mind, my scientific endeavours are pointless. Most intervention can be described as piecemeal contrivances which have no long-term beneficial influence when the real task should be prevention.

I started out discussing prevention and the common-sense approach to avoiding disorder in all its many guises at the psychological, physical and social levels. I have tried to point out the futility of science to come up with remedies without the practical simple application of prevention.

So, what needs to be done to prevent the growing numbers of children and adults who lack the foundational stability they need to get on and lead contented lives, who otherwise blame society and have a perpetual grudge that they have been dealt an unfair hand and feel, in Jake's own words, "They haven't the guts to fight?" Here are some suggestions:

- Children should not be born into families where they are at the mercy of instability, thwarting their psychological and educational development.
- Society needs to recognise the effects it has on families, undermining parental attempts to discipline, etc.
- Victims like Jake do not just need a prescribed medication, which cannot heal psychic pain: most of them already medicate themselves and use alcohol and drugs to numb their feelings.
- Children need understanding and trusting rehabilitation facilities which are consistent and manned by exceptional therapists.

The task is huge, but so are the consequences of not doing more. We owe these failed children (like Jake) help based on common sense and trust, rather than employing theoretical strategies which are clinical and detached from reality. A pill? In short, these children, who will become our future patients, need care, love and support, which only comes from steadfast foundations provided by families and schools, based on stability and trust. We need to fully understand their psychic pain.

Chapter 4
A potentially dangerous case study

One of my first cases at the family therapy unit was that of a family consisting of parents and their three children. This case was particularly difficult because the family was referred to the educational welfare department via the school, who were worried about the children's behaviour. One question obvious to the trained eye is: Why didn't the school contact the parents and share their concerns with them directly?

The answer becomes evident as this case unravels, but suffice it to say, the school was intuitively sensitive to the issue. Understandably, families who are in difficulty want to hide, minimise and deny difficulties to both the outside world and within the family itself.

Families found it much more acceptable to be referred by their family doctor, who they know must maintain confidentiality, as opposed to local authorities, such as social services and the school welfare department. Both of these entities have a statutory obligation to report certain cases to the authorities. If necessary, they can remove children from the home. As a therapist, I much preferred when the referral came from a doctor because then the doctor was the point of contact. It also implied that the patient had initiated it, which suggested that the family would work with you and go along with their doctor, whom they trusted.

In this particular case, the family did not have a GP, and they had already come up against the local authorities. In fact, the whole problem had been ignited by the local authorities failing to allow the family to build a house on a plot of land which they had purchased. As the case unravelled, it became clear that this was not the real cause of the problem; rather, the problem had its origins in the personality of the father, who had been born, lived and worked in London.

Under the guise of an apparently rational decision, the husband had persuaded his wife, Jen, that for the sake of their children's future, they needed to up sticks and move out of London, thereby providing a safer place for them to live with their children on Sussex coast. It is, of course, not unusual for people to try to solve their problems themselves by moving, etc. However, with mental illness and/or personality disorders, those solutions are often unrealistic and can compound the problem.

The referral came via an educational welfare officer to the department of family therapy: three children had recently moved to the area with their parents and they were causing concern at the school they attended. The children were hyperactive and disruptive in their classrooms. As I mentioned, it is of particular note that neither the school nor the school welfare officer spoke to the parents about their concerns for the children.

The referral information only provided a rough address, so it was not possible to make a telephone call to contact the family in the usual manner. That afternoon, I drove to a marshy area near a beach to a collection of derelict beach huts. It was the beginning of winter, with the wind blowing off the sea and the rain beating down. I was looking for a blue hut. In the end, I found a rather shabby hut with blue paint peeling off to expose the wet wood beneath. It was off the beaten track, surrounded by shrubs and had a rudimentary, uneven path made of brick rubble leading to an entrance. There were drab curtains drawn at the windows. It looked forlorn, bleak and damp. I picked my way along the path, not wanting to slip into the clay on either side. I tapped gently on the door and, after about five minutes, a woman partially opened it. She edged outside, shivering in the cold and shutting the door behind her. She wanted to find out who I was and what I wanted. It was obvious that she wanted to keep me outside of the hut. She seemed to be very wary and nervous. I explained to her that the school had some concerns about the children settling in and that I was calling to see if I could help. She apologised for leaving me outside in the cold and said she'd have to ask her husband. She did not feel able to make a decision to let me into the hut without consulting him.

I waited outside. A while later, she came out again, saying, "I am so sorry, but my husband does not want to see anyone from the authorities."

I began to explain to her that I quite understood, when a voice from inside shouted, "She can come in, Jen."

Jen visibly relaxed a little and invited me in. The only space was taken up by a double bed. Two up-ended orange boxes served as chairs and a very makeshift primus stove was in a corner. There was no evidence of, or space for, a tap or toilet inside, so I presumed they were elsewhere. It was beyond comprehension how a family of five could live in such cramped, difficult and unhealthy conditions, especially during the winter.

The woman introduced herself as Jen and said, "This is my husband, Dave."

Dave was lying on the bed covered in blankets. He was obviously a large man, was bespectacled with a black beard. I had the distinct feeling of being in the presence of – grandiosity! Dave took over, telling me his story while Jen put on the kettle, pouring water from a plastic drum to make tea. Jen was hunched up shivering against the cold. She was of average height with brown, dishevelled hair. She looked uncared for and miserable.

I learned that they were a Cockney family of five: one girl, aged five, and two boys, aged six and eight. The couple wanted a more natural life by the sea where their children could grow up safely out of the rat race, they told me. They came from London where Dave had worked as a docker. They had sold up in London and had purchased a piece of land, which they thought came with permission to build a house. However, once they had moved from London, it was revealed that the plot did not have the necessary planning permission. Desperate, the family dipped into their savings and purchased the blue hut with some of the money intended to build the house. At first sight, they appeared to be a well-intentioned couple wanting what was best for their children. However, as I became more informed, I realised that this was not the case.

The present

At the beginning of the autumn term, the children had to start attending a school, which was a statutory obligation. Without any form of transportation, the family needed to live within walking distance of a school. They had purchased the hut to tide them over. Jen did not talk, but I noticed that Dave would include her in the decisions they had made, saying 'we' when it was pretty obvious that Jen was not allowed to have any opinions of her own. Dave was not complaining or even concerned about the living arrangements, but I could see that, as winter set in, life had become impossible for Jen. There was no refrigerator or washing machine, and there was no television to occupy the children during the long, dark evenings – nothing. How Jen managed to feed, clothe and care for the family was difficult to imagine. Why Dave had taken to his bed was another issue.

Dave related how they (meaning him) didn't want contact with anyone and that he was against the children having friends. Jen interjected and said, "But, Dave, the school seems to be good, and the parents are welcoming."

Jen's comment provoked Dave into a furious outburst. In front of me, he said, "Jen, listen to me! How many times have I told you not to speak to anyone?"

She apologised, "Lots of times, Dave. I am so sorry."

"See what I have to put up with?" he appealed to me.

I could see quite clearly why the children were reacting. I could also see that Jen was in a miserable and precarious position, scared to provoke Dave. Life for her was only tolerable if she agreed with everything he said and reinforced his need to be dominant and admired. She was trying to appease her husband, on the one hand, and probably attempting to reason with the children, on the other, if they upset him. Such appalling conditions was a recipe for illness.

To be in a position to learn more and to help them, I needed to remain in contact with them – even if it meant appearing to collude by boosting Dave's ego. For this reason, I could not empathise or intervene on Jen's behalf; I couldn't confront. In a relatively short amount of time, Dave had shown his absolute lack of empathy and disregard for his wife. He was also naïve in believing that I did not see through his behaviour.

The situation initially called for practical management. I would usually consider paying a visit to the school; in this particular case, however, I decided this course of action would be unhelpful. If Dave found out that I had visited the school, any involvement with the family would certainly be stopped – of that I was sure. Initially, the aim was to manage the situation by getting treatment for Dave. If this could be achieved, I felt the children and Jen could respond quickly and positively.

The most pressing need was to maintain acceptance from both the parents. Needing more time to assess the situation, I said goodbye, suggesting that I would return. Judging by their reaction, that did not appear to be a problem, which felt like progress.

When I returned the next day, they appeared moderately pleased to see me. This time, I wanted to understand Dave and his psychopathology. It was not difficult to engage with him; he seemed to enjoy the attention. He talked animatedly about his childhood in London and being an only child. He particularly enjoyed pointing out his achievements and responsibilities as a docker. Jen would brighten up, nodding appreciatively; however, if she interjected, he would tell her not to interrupt and appeal to me by saying, "You see what I have to put up with?"

He recounted his work as a docker. More specifically, he stated that he was a crane driver and that he would spend every day high above London, loading and unloading the ships in the docks. I encouraged him by showing genuine interest and saying how responsible he was. At no time was it appropriate to talk to Jen or confront his controlling behaviour towards her. My role was to remain the only person outside the family to be accepted. They had not even registered with a local doctor, which was very unusual.

Dave described how he began to feel estranged from the world beneath when he was poised high above London in the crane. He explained that once he was in the crane, he had to remain in the cab until the end of the working day. He described that as he looked down from the cab, the world far below seemed to be hostile and in turmoil.

At some stage during this time in London, he began to persuade Jen that, to safeguard their family from this 'hostile' environment, they needed to cut all ties with their families in London and move to the safety of the seaside and country.

Depersonalisation, according to Ackner (1954), is described as feeling disconnected or estranged from one's body, thoughts or emotions; it is usually combined with narcissism and paranoia, which appeared to be what Dave was experiencing.

Suddenly, from happily recalling his achievements and aspirations and explaining his dream to escape from the world and its hostility, he switched to the present and said, "I want to kill the planning officer who turned down my plan to build a house." At that moment, this appeared to be a distinct possibility; it did not seem to be just an idle threat.

The children came home from school. When I showed some interest towards them, they began to talk about their day. Dave did not like me engaging with the children; he quickly turned on them and accused them of not helping him and of acting inappropriately. He went to demeaning lengths to make each one apologise and admit how inappropriate and bad their behaviour was. Jen looked on, too frightened and afraid to defend them and not knowing if I agreed with her husband or not.

During this altercation, Dave appeared to resent not being in the spotlight and kept looking at me, appealing for my support and sympathy. He then attacked Jen, blaming her for the bad behaviour of the children.

I left, once again, to reconsider the right path to take. There was no doubt in my mind as to the danger the family was in. The situation was precarious. It would only take some crisis to trigger an irretrievable reaction by Dave, such as one of the family members becoming ill – perhaps a child getting influenza or some such illness, which was a distinct possibility in the circumstances. Or of him killing the planning officer. Or even his family.

During a supervision session with the consultant child psychiatrist and other staff members, I said that I would like to discuss this particular family. I concluded by asking whether I should try to refer Dave to the adult psychiatric service. They asked the question: "Could anyone else do any better?" They were united in their opinion that I should not refer Dave for treatment. I gave considerable thought to their view but decided that the situation was severe and merited the right action. This was a risky move on my part. At the time, there appeared to be an unwritten rule within the Family Therapy Centre that one didn't refer to the adult service. I was not a party to the reason why this was, but I suspected it could have been based on rivalry.

I decided to go against my colleagues and contact the psychiatrist responsible for the catchment area in which the family lived. This was a risk I was willing to take; for me, losing my job was not as important as the distinct possibility of the murder of the planning officer. The adult psychiatrist in charge of the area was relaxed, and he suggested that he accompany me on a domiciliary visit. I felt I needed to pave the way for the visit, so once again, I visited the couple and Dave, and I talked while Jen hovered and listened, clearly very nervous. It was quite evident that as Dave realised the precariousness of the family's circumstances, the situation had become more dangerous. As I have said, I never confronted Dave. Moreover, he never admitted any responsibility for the situation, but he did appear to acknowledge that he needed help and that the situation was unsustainable.

Once I realised this, my fear was how he might act in these dire circumstances: he might kill himself, the planning officer or even his family. Whenever he lost face, he became very aggressive and desperate, feeling cornered. With a considerable degree of trepidation and having first enlisted the involvement of the psychiatrist unbeknown to Dave or Jen, I suggested that we invite a doctor to visit (I never said psychiatrist). I went on to explain that a doctor could make some helpful suggestions and may provide some help.

Jen became visibly scared; this was clearly a step too far for her.

Eventually, Dave said, "I'll go along with that." His agreement was on his terms, in his home, proving he was in control. What's more, the attention was on helping him!

I was nervous. I didn't know the psychiatrist, and, although I respected his expertise, I needed to warn him about the precarious nature of the situation. I wanted to maintain the inroads I had made so far with Dave. The psychiatrist was understanding and appeared not to resent my cautious attitude. We decided to play down our respective roles by travelling the last few hundred yards to the blue hut in one car. We both agreed that the whole consultation needed to be as low-key as possible. The psychiatrist took the initiative and knocked on the door. He then peeped inside – he was used to this kind of situation.

"Anyone home?" he asked. Seeing there was no room for four in the hut, he suggested we sit in his car. Dave came outside in his pyjamas and wrapped in a blanket. He sat in the front seat of the car with a discernible grandiose demeanour while I sat in the back. The psychiatrist skilfully engaged with him and listened while Dave told him the story. Dave concluded by saying, "I aim to kill the planning officer."

Deferring to Dave for his agreement, the psychiatrist suggested that we needed to confer alone to discuss what help could be offered. Dave agreed and returned to the hut, leaving us in the car. The psychiatrist thought Dave was a threat to himself, the family and the planning officer, and that he should be in the hospital. We both felt, if possible, Dave should go to the hospital as a voluntary patient. It was left to me to try to persuade Dave (the alternative was a compulsion order). This meant that if Dave failed to agree to go to the hospital voluntarily, then the psychiatrist would sign the necessary papers with the mental welfare officer. Moreover, he would advise the officer to take the police with him. The psychiatrist also said he wanted the children to be away (preferably at school) if this happened. We were both worried about Jen. The psychiatrist left, having arranged for Dave's admission that evening or the next morning. I went back to the hut and explained to Dave and Jen that the doctor suggested a short spell in hospital to help him regain his health. Somewhat shocked, Dave took the news surprisingly well: he agreed.

He was given a bed for the next day. I rang the ward before setting out to collect Dave to explain to the charge nurse that the situation was volatile. I explained that if Dave was respected and perhaps offered tea on arrival, this was the best chance of success. Dave was ready when I arrived, and we left, with Jen waving him off but upset. I could have arranged an ambulance, but I did not want to risk him changing his mind, feeling that any minor upset could have led to his refusal to go to the hospital voluntarily. Dave had shown that he could change from being affable one second to menacing the next. Because everything was working out, perhaps too easily, the thought crossed my mind that Dave was playing along. For all I knew, he might have drawn a gun and shot me before absconding with my car. However, the journey turned out to be uneventful.

I became apprehensive again when we drove through the entrance of the psychiatric hospital, fearing that something might suddenly alert him to where we were going. Mentally ill patients can behave strangely; only the week before, a patient had lain right across the entrance to the hospital so that everyone had to step around her. I just hoped that something similar wouldn't happen this day. We walked down the long corridor, our footsteps echoing annoyingly. We came to the ward, and thankfully, the door was unlocked. The staff were on the alert and welcomed Dave with tea. I left after Dave had been admitted, relieved that we had gotten this far. My job now was to return to Jen and talk with her, something I had felt was inappropriate in the company of Dave.

Jen was very motherly and charming and would make very cold milky tea and stir honey in it for nutrition. The other memory I have of Jen is that she would buy rolls at a corner shop and slices of ham and would make a roll for me, pointing out it had butter as well as ham, as if it were a real treat. She only had ham. She was wonderful, never complaining, just grateful that things were changing for the better. I took Jen to visit Dave during his time in the hospital. He was doing very well, proud to be helping the other patients with 'advice'. He was discharged three weeks later, stabilised.

The next step was to get Dave earning again, but jobs in this area were few and far between. In the UK at this time, companies by law needed to employ a quota of physically challenged employees. Once Dave was at home, I was able to persuade him that this route would be the easiest way for him to obtain employment. He did not like the idea at first, but he gradually came around to seeing the advantages. I made contact with a company which wanted security staff to man the entrance to a famous factory. The job entailed checking security and people going into the company by operating a gate and waving people through once they had shown their passes. This position was ideal and met all of Dave's needs: he was required to wear a uniform, he was in control, he commanded respect and he was once again the breadwinner. He took his work very seriously, and the company was delighted with him. His symptoms subsided, and he became more affable. The couple was able to secure a mortgage and buy a shop with living accommodations above. Jen made the shop a great success, and everyone loved her. The children settled at school and were integrated well into the community.

Summary

In retrospect, and reconsidering the dynamics, Dave's problems were most probably precipitated when he was isolated in the crane high above London. His absence of empathy led to speculations about the nature of his narcissistic disorder and the accompanying grandiosity that must have existed before. In all probability, anyone with a reasonably balanced personality would not have become disordered in similar circumstances. The appeal of working in the crane cab in isolation may have been a consequence of his personality disorder; he was at the top of the hierarchy while working. Finding another job within the dockyard, once he became depersonalised, was the most obvious solution and the least extreme, but Dave would not have pursued this option and would have found it demeaning.

Such a personality needed to be reined in or disciplined from an early age, but as an only child adored by his parents, this never happened. Dave was now a large, powerful docker, not someone with whom to cross swords. He didn't socialise or mix well with his workmates. Jen never confronted him and played an entirely subservient and submissive role. She was the antipathy of Dave and possibly had been selected by him for that very reason.

The risks involved in this particular case were not for everyone. The case could have been referred to social services, who would have dealt with it differently, most likely by taking the children into care. Alternatively, Dave could have been allocated to the psychiatric services; however, the behaviour of the children was the only visible indication that the family was in trouble, and the children's hyperactivity was the cause of the referral.

The psychiatrist commented afterward that if the case had been referred to him, he would have spent less time with Dave, and he would have called for outside help, which may have provoked Dave into becoming hostile and less cooperative in the ward. He may have even killed someone. Moreover, Dave would not have been supported after discharge from the hospital. I was a family therapist, and my background in rehabilitation influenced my attitude towards the management of the case and my personal intervention to get him a job.

I moved on, and I did not have the opportunity to check up on the family again. Years later, when I coincidently happened to read the obituaries column in the local press, I found one for Jen. She had died of cancer at just 54 years old. This news immediately rekindled my research (Thomson, 1996) on the causal relationships between premature deaths following a depressive illness, considering Selye's (1974) stress hypothesis and my own research on stress and personality (Thomson, nee Evans, 1981). Other research reported that

> Cancer-prone people, as opposed to coronary heart disease prone people tend to be overly cooperative, appeasing, unassertive, over-patient, avoiding conflict and seek harmony. They are compliant, defensive, suppress the expression of emotion and are unable to deal with interpersonal stress, which leads to feelings of hopelessness/helplessness and finally depression. (Grossarth-Maticek & Eysenck, 1989)

In turn, this leads to high cortisol levels and immune deficiencies, and I wondered if cancer was the real cause of Jen's death or a secondary outcome to a life of complete subordination.

It would have been so easy to presume that with the children doing well in school, with Dave happy at his job and with Jen successfully running the shop, the intervention had been successful; however, in my opinion, it had not been. Sadly, Jen continued to be bullied and subservient, always on tenterhooks. She would have been the recipient of unrelenting psychological stress associated with Dave's personality. My research and my experience, together with the close contact I had with the family, led me to believe that Dave's personality was an important causal factor of Jen's premature death.

The difficulty I had, in this case, was also the rivalry which existed between the adult psychiatric service and the family therapy unit. When I presented this case for supervision, there was a concerted pressure from my fellow family therapists for me to not refer Dave to adult services. This was alienating since I decided that the seriousness of the case justified the referral. These tensions within a psychotherapeutic group must be confronted to enable therapists to be both creative and effective in bringing about change. I realised that if anything had gone wrong, I risked losing my job and having an accusatory finger pointed at me for any consequences. If there are difficulties in the relationships within a therapeutic unit, then there is an argument that it may be unable to succeed at the core activity for which it owes its existence and purpose.

Having worked in both general psychiatry and in family therapy, I have considered the potential benefits of these two disciplines working together, but I never enjoyed this in reality. In fact, as I explained, while trying to achieve this, I found myself in an uncomfortable position. In general psychiatry, the family were never considered to be sick. In group psychotherapy, for example, I witnessed patients denigrating and placing the blame on a partner, mother, father or sibling, but no one corroborated these accusations; they were taken at face value. It was, therefore, so easy to be misguided and jeopardise treatment objectives. Only in family therapy was the whole story considered. As these cases exemplify, the children were made the scapegoats. How wrong it would have been to collude with Mrs Smith and have Veronica condemned as a wicked dirty child (the next case). So, I hope that anyone playing a major role in the lives of patients will have an understanding of the family dynamics and identify where the root of the psychopathology really lies.

Chapter 5

Veronica, or Personality Disorders in the Parents of Children with Emotional Disorders

There are parallels between the previous two cases and the one that is described in this chapter: the children were the referral source, but the central characters needing managing were the parents. The parents were lonely, anti-authority, un-empathic, manipulative and aggressive when thwarted. They used their families towards their own ends, all of which indicated undiagnosed personality disorders. They had captive partners who were compliant and impotent. As will be described below.

Mrs Smith was notorious for getting her own way. She had threatened to dump dirty sheets on the steps of the town hall if she were denied a clothes dryer. Suffice it to say, social services buckled under the pressure and provided her with one. In both cases, Dave and Mrs Smith needed from me a similar degree of delicacy and diplomacy, and there was a lot at stake for both the children and the families if things went wrong and if I didn't make a difference.

In the case before us, Veronica suffered from enuresis caused by the emotional stress she endured as a scapegoat, which was initiated and condoned by her mother, Mrs Smith. The enuresis provided Mrs Smith with the evidence she needed to persuade others that Veronica was a dirty child who should be removed from the family and put into care.

Veronica's mother, like Dave, was also very anti-authority. She could not forgive the hospital for sterilising her and denying her the regular holiday she had in hospital when having another baby. She truly believed that not only was she being denied the pleasure but so were the nurses at the local hospital, who, according to Mrs Smith, relished her admission. Mrs Smith always had a campaign, the present one being a bell and pad (as mentioned above), and following this, it was the complete rejection of Veronica and persuading social services to take her into its care. The problem was that Mrs Smith was becoming very skilled at these campaigns; she was never going to lose. Her husband was similar to Jen and was very compliant. He lay on a couch, nursing his broken leg, his big eyes looking at the family, no doubt oblivious as to what was happening because his reality was blurred by epileptic drugs. He was completely overawed by his wife.

However, in these various cases where the children were referred as the patients needing treatment, I began to wonder if the parents themselves had been victims of abuse similar to scapegoating. I could clearly identify these parents as presently displaying behaviour associated with a personality disorder and that they should be identified as the patient. Nevertheless, they were, perhaps, themselves victims. One of the patients told me that she was merely replicating the same behaviour as her mother and grandmother had exhibited before. She was inferring that her problems were genetic and that she was vulnerable. If she was right, the link needed to be broken, and clearly, it was up to psychotherapeutic intervention to break the cycle. Of course, this brings into question the stance of the psychiatrist who refused to treat personality disorders (as in the case of Adele, who will be discussed below), which implied the cyclic behaviour replicated from one generation to the next cannot be stopped.

Anyway, back to Mrs Smith. The GP referral read: *Please, can I refer this child. The mother is requesting a bell and pad for her eight-year-old daughter, Veronica, to stop her enuresis. The mother has a heart condition, and her third husband, who is an epileptic, has recently fallen from a ladder while working as a painter and broken his leg. There are four children, ages ranging from four to eight, and Veronica is the eldest. The children have different fathers.*

I took the referral and followed the usual procedure: a telephone call was made to set up an initial appointment to visit the home. The family lived on an estate in local council accommodation. My first impressions were of the neatness of the house and garden in comparison to those of the neighbours. I decided to walk to the back door, which I could see was open at the top, being a stable-type door. Further up the garden, there were many sheets billowing in the wind. I tapped on the door, and Mrs Smith looked up from her ironing.

"You from the social?" she asked. "'Cause if you are, you can go – I don't want anything to do with you."

"No, I'm from family therapy. I've come because you requested a bell and pad."

"I just want it. I don't want advice or talking or anything else."

"I'm sorry, but I can't just provide one without knowing more about Veronica."

"Look at that line! Every day I'm washing and ironing. It ain't right. She's a filthy child. She should be put in a home," Mrs Smith said, fixing me with her dark-brown eyes. I was sympathetic as we talked about the problem of washing and drying the linen, and she said how social services had provided a clothes dryer. "Would you like to come in and have a cup of tea?" she invited.

"Well, that would be nice, but will it interrupt your ironing?"

She unlatched the door and let me into her home, which was spotless. I listened while she told me about herself. She was very angry because the only holiday she got was when she went into the hospital to have a baby. That luxury had now been denied her because, "They tied my tubes when I had my last without me knowing, because of my heart. The nurses will be upset because they enjoyed having me in the hospital." Over tea, she told me her troubles and how she had to cope with her husband recovering from the fall with no prospects of getting work.

Before I left, I said that I would need to see the family together. By then, she had warmed towards me, and I was able to tell her what would happen (i.e. sitting in a circle without the TV or any distractions would enable me to understand the family). I could see that Mrs Smith was, in some important ways, a devoted mother; she had high standards for running her home.

The day of the family session arrived, and it was beautifully prepared. There were chairs arranged in a circle with the husband lying on a couch at one end. The younger children were doing handstands in the middle, trying to dissipate the seriousness of the occasion. They took their places on the various chairs and waited expectantly, with one exception – a small, delicate girl outside the circle hovered behind me like a shadow, excluded.

I began the session by going around the circle, interested to hear the family talk about school and home life or whatever else they chose to tell me. Mrs Smith asked if everyone would like a drink and biscuits. Yes, they all shouted, as if it were a party, and Mrs Smith went to the kitchen.

The little girl, Veronica, who I decided was the patient, tapped me gently on the arm. She had a book in her hand. Her touch coincided with Mrs Smith returning with a tray of drinks and biscuits. "The lady doesn't want anything to do with a filthy girl like you," she said viciously. The remaining three children all retched and pretended to vomit, following this up with, "She smells." Veronica retreated, and sometime later, as we were disbanding, and by which time, I had reached my own conclusions, she persisted once again by tapping my arm, wanting to show me her book – it was *Cinderella.*

Veronica's father had abandoned Mrs Smith, and Veronica herself was very beautiful – quite unlike her mother and stepbrother and sisters. Mrs Smith projected all her problems and prejudices onto the child, believing that if Veronica were removed, all of her problems would be solved. Veronica was Cinderella.

The main purpose of researching this case and the other cases reported in 'Manikins Nursery Rhymes and Secrets' (discussed below) was to determine if other therapists had experienced the way the children were using various methods to explain their problems. I found it very interesting; however, the main difficulty, in this case, was turning around the very vicious relationship between Veronica and her family. Veronica was deteriorating and losing the space to develop normally, and she was not thriving educationally. This had similarities to the situation of Dave's family in the beach hut: I had to help Mrs Smith in order to help Veronica.

Mrs Smith was impatient and shrewd enough to realise that I was not going to provide the bell and pad immediately, so I had to make progress quickly. My first visit, after the initial family session, was to the school. The school thought of Veronica as a child with learning difficulties, and they were right – to a point. But would she have had those difficulties if she came from a secure and loving family? My hunch was that she would not. I left the school pleased that at least Veronica was not bullied and that the staff treated her kindly without expecting too much from her, which removed any pressure while she was at school. However, Veronica looked ill: she had the hollow eyes and pale complexion so typical of children under severe stress.

My next step was to engineer a loving relationship between Mrs Smith and Veronica. Mrs Smith was quite a caring mother, but she needed attention, and she resented the attention Veronica was receiving. My plan was to give her attention, which was contingent upon Veronica. I decided that Mrs Smith needed to enjoy an adventure with Veronica, so we all went to an excursion to the cathedral city, unfamiliar event, which involved a ride in my car and coffee and cake. We walked to the Market Cross which stands at the centre of the city and is believed to have been built in 1501. We marvelled that Bishop Edward Story paid ten pounds to the Mayor of Chichester for the ground on which it is built. This went very well, and they both enjoyed this rare treat. I then suggested that Mrs Smith teach Veronica to knit, so we purchased wool and needles. I drove them both home and said that I would call to see how they were getting on. Mrs Smith was now the therapist, and this simple and cost-effective plan worked well. Veronica would show me her knitting, and Mrs Smith prided herself on being a good teacher.

I also took Mrs Smith to the school Veronica attended, and she relished the opportunity to be respected by the staff. The staff, in turn, provided material for homework, and Mrs Smith took this new responsibility very seriously. My role diminished as Veronica began to improve, and the relationship became that of a proud mother keen to promote her daughter and not a vicious mother whose sole preoccupation was scapegoating her daughter and engineering her placement in a children's home. Veronica responded very quickly by stopping the bed-wetting and catching up at school educationally. I hoped that, eventually, she would leave the special school and attend a normal school and attain her potential.

However, the key to success was overcoming the resentment felt by Mrs Smith about her stay in hospital being denied her by not being able to have another child and having three husbands who had fallen short in some way. She had learnt to manipulate very successfully. Her life had been spent cultivating this ability not to be thwarted by anyone. It had become a skill. I have seen this in many patients if they are not working for various reasons. They have all the time in the world to plot and instigate and justify a stance on some bandwagon. Employment is cost-effective in such cases. The biblical book of Proverbs comes to mind: 'Idle hands are the devil's workshop; idle lips are his mouthpiece. An evil person sows strife; gossip separates the best of friends. Wickedness loves' (16:27–29 TLB).

Veronica was a fragile, emotionally ill child; however, what I learned was that her fragility did not prevent her from persistently trying to show me her *Cinderella* book. She did this despite risking more vicious attacks from her brother and sister and more punishment and degradation from her mother. I found this astounding. My experience with Veronica is included in the next chapter, which explores the intricate features of this type of situation and interaction. It was due to Veronica's insistence and perseverance that I became fascinated by the insights which I would like to share.

Chapter 6
Manikins, Nursery Rhymes and Secrets

C G Jung tells how as a child he had a hoard of secrets, including a stone and a small manikin, which he would sneak a look at when there was an undercurrent of trouble between his parents. Similarly, as a family therapist, I sometimes found the children referred to the Family Therapy Service – and it was always the children – would connect with me using these various means to explain their unexplainable, their psychic pain.

Jung's analytical psychology set him apart from the mainstream. For him, the diagnosis was important only for the doctors and was not considered helpful to the patient. He studied the deeper aspects of human psychology through the study of religious beliefs, dreams, myths, symbols and the paranormal. The following cases are just some of the many interactions which I think have resonance with Jung.

I received this request from a GP: *Please, would you see this little boy. Nursery school is worried about his behaviour.*

I rang to make an appointment to see the family together. The family turned out to be a girl, aged six, a boy, aged four, and his mother, all living together in a very nice bungalow. The father had left to live with another woman. The daughter was at school, but the little boy was at home with his mother when I called. It is always a tell-tale sign when children won't leave to play but stay nearby as if they have to be present and vigilant for any meeting because it is too important to miss.

The mother said she was beside herself with worry as the husband wanted to sell the family home. When he had first told her he was leaving her, he had said she could keep the home. She was clearly depressed – limp and pale and trying to put a brave face on the situation. The bungalow was cold and bleak – she had to turn down the heating to save costs. She apologised to be telling me of her own predicament when I had come about concerns with her little boy. Clearly, she made no connection between her own desperation and that of her son.

The little boy had the customary hollowed eyes of a troubled child, and he was pale but lively and hyperactive. He was very intent on this unusual visitor and the interactions between her and his mother that was happening in his home. He wouldn't play; he just listened attentively.

His mother asked me if I would like tea and, as this is always a positive suggestion, I generally accept.

While his mother was in the kitchen making the tea, the little boy became very active and purposeful: he went out of the room and returned with a ladder. Somewhat alarmed, I tried to caution him, but he, very hurriedly, climbed the ladder, felt along the edge of a bureau, climbed down and quickly gave me a small box, at which point, his mother came in with the tea.

"What on earth have you been up to?" she asked him, clearly both bewildered and embarrassed.

Another symbol. In the box was his mother's wedding ring, which was no longer on her finger. In this case, I could not interview the father, but once again, this little boy exhibited the same purposefulness of Veronica, retrieving an object that was weighted with symbolism related to his predicament. This was not an easy case because the divorce proceedings were prolonged, and the mother was unable to pay for the legal representation that she needed. My role was to support her throughout the process and pull whatever strings I could from my own network.

Referral 3

The school doctor referred a child, a little boy of five: "This child is behind in his usual milestones. Can you assess?"

Following the same procedure, I arranged to meet with the family. The mother was a hairdresser, the father a draughtsman. There was a girl of ten, and the little boy who was five. Once again, the boy appeared delicate, pale and withdrawn. His mother took the lead and the father agreed with what she said, namely, that they were shocked that he had been referred and were very worried because the school wondered if he was retarded.

I decided to return and see the mother on her own some days later. She told me she hadn't left the house since she had had the little boy because she was agoraphobic, for which she had been prescribed Valium by her GP. The little boy had spent a great proportion of his early life constricted at home, sharing his mother's fears and limitations.

I was amazed at how skilful the mother was. She had a rota of friends who would enable her to remain in the home by shopping, doing errands, etc. The husband had become so accustomed to this unusual situation that he didn't question how restricted family life was.

I started visiting her, and once the process of her treatment was started, the family began to readjust. The little boy very quickly began attending school and, far from being retarded, was very bright.

The mother would relate to nursery rhymes to explain how she felt, such as being the 'farmer's wife' from the playground game, *The Farmer Wants a Wife*. Another example was the *Billy Goats Gruff* and the *Three Little Pigs*. The wolf in the story of *Red Riding Hood* was another character that was used. Our sessions were spent relating and applying the dynamics of the games and rhymes to her own position and the alternatives.

Four months into the treatment, the mother discussed with me her decision to stop taking Valium. I suggested she speak to her doctor, fearful that she needed supervision. Despite suffering very severe withdrawal symptoms, she persevered. She was also walking to the hairdressing salon where she had worked five years previously and had begun working for two hours a day.

I do not include the details of treatment in the published case reports. The focus of this section is to share the importance the children gave to manikins, symbols, nursery rhymes and secrets. I hope this conveys the underlining and very intuitive interactions through which the children engaged in my intervention within the family. It goes without saying that ours were special relationships, in which sanctity and trust played a crucial role during interactions with families.

However, all families were discharged successfully within six months of referral. The children appeared to become secure through an intuitive appreciation that someone had taken on their burdens. In all cases, the behaviour of the children, in terms of attention span, hyperactivity and general well-being, improved quite rapidly. I should also note that working in cooperation with schools was vitally important as teachers sometimes punished the children for what was merely the children's reactions to extreme family turmoil and intolerable circumstances. Naturally, teachers needed to appreciate what the children were experiencing out of school and to educate themselves to look at the children with new eyes, viewing them with kindness and understanding rather than offering punishment. Part of my job was to offer support and educate the teachers. To involve the family, including the grandparents, brothers, sisters and the school teachers in the treatments and then praise them for subsequent progress was all part of turning these cases around as quickly as possible to ensure that everyone felt a sense of achievement.

The next case involved a similar family, and the child who was referred had a dominant, non-empathetic, anti-authoritarian father. The referral from the family's GP read: *Please, can you take this referral? Six-year-old Simon and his parents are in serious disagreement on a way forward. He is now in trouble with the police for stealing.* I contacted the mother to arrange a meeting with the family, but the father was at sea and the remaining three sons had left home.

The mother wanted to see me alone. When I met her, she was distraught: Simon had been caught stealing small objects from shops on numerous occasions. The local police had been asked by the father to threaten him and teach him a lesson. The mother's view was that Simon was a lovely little boy who acted as her protector while his father was away at sea, but when his father came home, they did not get on. She didn't know why he stole despite knowing the threats and risks he would encounter if he continued to steal. His brothers were all doing well and loved Simon, but this was something they had never encountered before: a thief in the midst of a very law-abiding family, and they were very ashamed.

I met Simon alone, and we formed a mutually warm and trusting relationship. Like so many little boys, he had become the surrogate husband to his mother. He did not understand the family dynamics and certainly was too young to enunciate his emotional turmoil. While his father was at sea, Simon and his mother were supportive of each other, but when the father came home, he had to revert to being a little boy. When we discussed what he stole, he told me he stole little men and tiny cars and kept them in a secret place. When he was in trouble, he would go to this secret place and play with the stolen items. They had no value, and he could have easily bought these items with his pocket money.

When the father came back from sea, he joined his wife in an appointment with me. He told me that he was against his son and wife getting outside help and that what I had to offer was waffle, a waste of time! In his opinion, his son needed a good beating. I listened and suggested he give me some time: I guaranteed we would resolve Simon's unacceptable behaviour.

Like Veronica, Simon risked a beating from his father and a visit from the village policeman for stealing the manikins he had hidden away as a source of private comfort. Simon eventually stopped stealing once I was able to influence the situation, but in each case, I did not treat the children – I had to remedy the behaviour and feelings of the parents. In Simon's case, the father resented the close relationship between his wife and his son, and he needed to realise that his wife was beginning to dread his homecoming. The breakthrough came after sessions with Simon's parents while the father was on leave. And once again, it was relatively easy to orchestrate a change in the relationship between Simon and his father. After a while, the father agreed to take Simon out fishing, and the relationship between them began to heal by focusing on the joint activity. Simon never stole again.

My predecessor at the family therapy unit was a play therapist. The playroom that he used became my room, and I resented the mess. On the walls were daubs of coloured paint, which were also on the carpet. There was a sand tray in the corner and other playthings littered around. After the initial difficulties I experienced as the new therapist, and once I found my stride, I wondered if I would ever resort to using these playthings and techniques to resolve my cases and treat the children. Because I had only found the children reacting to the personality disorders of the parents, I had very little to do with the children who were referred for treatment. It seemed that once the problem had become identified, the children very quickly improved, and the speed of their progress was amazing. In comparison, while psychiatric patients were often subjected to prolonged treatment after diagnosis, the children improved in a week. Perhaps they felt intuitively released to get on with life and be children, safe in the knowledge that the unexplained was taken care of. Another salient factor was seeing families in their own homes with very few exceptions. If I hadn't had such access, I would not have become aware of the clues and family dynamics which led me towards understanding and solving these cases.

It was through seeing the children in their family environments that led me to an important insight regarding their use of symbols!

I was excited to know whether others involved in therapeutic intervention experienced the same phenomena. Veronica really intrigued me; despite her fragility, she persisted in showing me her precious *Cinderella* book. Without referral notes or any other information, I could look at her as a very ill child with her book clenched to her chest and know all I needed to know. Other examples followed, including the cases above.

One day, I was driving along and suddenly, like a bolt of lightning, I came to the realisation that these children were producing symbols which conceptualised their predicament! It was so exciting, I even began expecting other children to produce these symbols: the ring, the *Cinderella* book, manikins, etc. At the next supervision, I dared to disclose the flash of lightning experience I had had. The psychiatrist responded by asking everyone else what was I experiencing. No one knew I learnt from him it was insight.

There were two elements associated with the insight. The one was personal to me – the sudden impact. The second was that these children had no means of explaining the seat of their psychic pain. So, it seemed this was an innate, tangible means: a shorthand diagnosis which they were using! Veronica was Cinderella. The ring symbolised the marriage breakdown. The manikins were the secret pain. And the nursery rhymes removed the pain from the patient to something manageable, almost regressive. Strangely, I observed that the agoraphobic patient was always smiling. She was managing to explain even her illness, her condition, in a light-hearted, acceptable, jovial manner via supposedly harmless entertaining children's rhymes, albeit with a sinister message. This patient was very attractive. A pregnancy had ensured she remained faithful to her husband, but once she had had her last child, completing her family, she knew she was vulnerable to temptation. Another method of ensuring her fidelity was to become agoraphobic and remain in the family home.

The case which is presented in the next chapter was unusual and managing it was a challenge. Unlike most referrals involving an emotional illness in a child, where usually the initial diagnosis is retardation and failure to reach developmental milestones, in this next case, the roles were reversed: the parents were not as bright as their son.

Chapter 7
"I've Got the Answer!"

Paul, a boy of eight, was referred to the family therapy centre by his GP for encopresis of six months' duration. Unbeknown to me, because of the seriousness of the diagnosis, a referral had previously been made to a regional children's unit where an appointment had been arranged for three months' time.

For those unacquainted with encopresis, it is when children soil their underwear after the age of four, by which time, usually, they have been toilet-trained. Additionally, they may smear the faeces on walls and contaminate surfaces and clothing. Encopresis is considered a very severe form of disturbance in children. It can arise in some children as a response to a stressful situation. Some research has associated encopresis with sexual abuse. Encopresis can also reflect poor parent-child relationships, often longstanding and usually associated with other aspects of psychiatric disturbance.

I made an appointment to visit the family at home. They lived in a small country village where Paul went to school locally. Unusually, Paul opened the door and invited me into a small well-kept cottage. He introduced me to his parents, who were clearly in fear of my visit. The mother dived in to explain that Paul was soiling himself at home and at school. She showed me the washing on the line outside drying and led me into the small scullery. Inside were sheets soaking in the sink and clothes were in various buckets. The father looked on nervously, smiling benevolently while his wife showed her disgust. She gave the impression that it wasn't her problem anymore and looked to me to do something – here was the inconvertible evidence! Paul hovered in the background with his hands in his pockets, waiting for my conclusion, as if he too were looking for a remedy.

We moved into a small living room where Paul's mother talked about their life, and how Paul's parents and grandparents had all worked locally, never travelling far beyond the village. They were clearly hard-working country folk who took pleasure and pride in living simply. Paul's mother kept referring to the grandparents, saying that they were stunned and distraught by the problem. Paul, as the only son and grandson, appeared to be central to all their lives, and his encopresis was obviously a shock which they all shared but could not understand or tolerate. Paul had, it seemed, slipped from being exalted to being an unprecedented conundrum in the family.

On that first visit, I got the impression from Paul that the soiling problem did not appear to have any emotional impact such as guilt or shame but something which just happened, like getting mumps or measles. The mother was the spokesperson and reflected predominantly the annoyance of the family. I suspected that the grandparents were an absent force to be reckoned with, goading her into doing something about it. So exasperated was Paul's mother on that first visit that she issued an ultimatum: "From this day, Paul will have to wash his own clothes and bedding!" She looked at me menacingly, as if to say take that! I felt like a mechanic employed to fix a car that wouldn't start and that, nevertheless, it was my fault and was now my responsibility.

I made another appointment and returned once again to be greeted by Paul. This time, he was on his own, which I suspected was deliberate because his parents had decided to absent themselves from what was now my problem. All these observations are important in family therapy, like the manikins etc., they were salient and indicative.

Paul appeared quite excited, saying, "I've got the answer! Come with me." Interested to hear about the answer, I followed him to the scullery and he showed me a bucket and a box labelled Bio-active! He explained to me that all he had to do was to measure out the correct amount of Bio-active into a bucket of water, stir it and leave the clothes to soak. Problem solved!

I was interested to learn how he came up with his solution since he only had access to a small village shop. He told me he had read the laundry products for sale in the shop and had paid for it with his pocket money. There was something amusing about Paul's attitude. He was managing the problem in an unemotional, detached but practical manner, in some ways similar to his mother's detached and unrealistic standpoint. Naturally, most children would find different and more enjoyable ways to spend their pocket money, but he was excited to have found what he thought was the solution!

I needed to find out more. I was interested to go beyond the soiling. I made an appointment to visit Paul's school. The headmaster had arranged for Paul's class teacher to join us in her coffee break. They saw it as a classroom difficulty, managing the soiling within a class of some thirty children was a practical problem. The teacher explained that Paul had to sit at a desk on his own in a small annex adjoining the main classroom, but he was unpopular because of the smell and the mess. For his teacher, it was managing the class of children and the mess so that she could teach. A cleaner had been made responsible for cleaning up the mess, and she had a stock of underpants provided by Paul's mother. Unless something changed, the management system would remain in place as the school staff felt everything was working well and was under control.

This again was a way of adapting, similar to the agoraphobic hairdresser discussed above. Her husband, parents and friends were all settled into their respective roles of helping her remain in a severely limited way of life. No one ever appeared to suggest a remedy. This collusive behaviour had to be exchanged for normality.

We discussed Paul and his attitude. The teacher's saw the soiling as a problem that needed practical management. She explained that Paul appeared quite adjusted to it, working alone in the annex and although not popular, he wasn't unpopular with the children, who tolerated the soiling. He wasn't bullied; in fact, his self-reliance attracted children to him on the one hand, while the smell and mess repelled them on the other.

I left feeling the school was a good, caring school which had not punished Paul, but had worked out how to deal with, what to them, needed a management solution.

Therapy

I needed now to work with Paul. I was increasingly of the opinion that Paul was bright, probably brighter than average and definitely brighter than his family. Up until now, everyone had colluded by dealing with the mess once it had been created, which historically was how the family, and now the school, coped with issues. I saw my job as concentrating on change. What was the mess? I had the strong impression that the family were reliant on Paul for his acumen. Now that this reliance was in jeopardy, he was in danger of being ostracised both at school and at home, but neither he nor the family could stop the soiling. The parents, and I presumed the grandparents, were in awe of him. To some extent, he was influencing the school and his home, and their reaction and management of the problem. At school, he was removed from the class and his contemporaries. At home, he was no longer revered beyond his eight years.

I gave considerable thought to the abnormal situation and came to the conclusion that the soiling was regressive because he wasn't ready to be an adult. If I was right, my task was to help him as the child but reinforce his capacity for growth, using the cooperation of those who could best promote that growth. From that day, I never mentioned the soiling, seeing it for what it was: a symptom of an emotionally disturbed, misunderstood child.

Using myself in the first instance before enlisting the help of the school and the education system was the strategy. This strategy was based on the fact that Paul's difficulty centred around his level of intellectual functioning, which was much superior to that of his family.

I hadn't appreciated how socially impoverished the family were, but I learnt that they hardly ever left the village. Paul had never been to the main town some six miles away. I decided to take him on an outing to a nearby city and castle. He absorbed everything: the car, the journey, the history, the orange squash and cake. The trip gave me the opportunity to get to understand him without seemingly interrogating him. I wanted to know more about his interests, his thought processes, his dreams and aspirations.

When I asked him what he most wanted to do, he surprised me by saying he wanted to play a musical instrument, particularly the cello. I revisited the school and discretely aired my view that Paul was a bright boy who was caught in a dilemma, exalted at home beyond his years. The teacher became interested and shared how Paul was now progressing in the classroom, suggesting his potential hadn't been realised before. I kept visiting the home and provided encouragement and support for the parents, and indirectly to the grandparents, who, although I had never met them, were clearly revered by Paul's parents.

I contacted the local musical education department and discussed the possibility of Paul loaning a cello and having music lessons at his school. Paul was delighted and volunteered to pay for the cello out of his pocket money. His parents were both dumbfounded and frightened by the news. They needed support to provide Paul with the necessary encouragement. It was a huge and frightening progression for them.

Paul began his cello lessons in earnest, much to the admiration of everyone. He progressed rapidly, practising at home, with his parents in awe of their son. The music stand and cello were on display all the time, enabling him to pick it up and practise whenever he wanted to, which was the key to progressing rapidly. The culmination of this was that he was asked by the headmaster to play a solo in the school assembly, to which, his family were invited. I made sure Paul's parents appreciated the part they had played in his recovery by not thwarting his ambition and by allowing him the space and time to practise. Paul's soiling had become a thing of the past.

Postscript

In the meantime, Paul was making progress and he had stopped soiling. I was invited with the parents to attend the consultation which had previously been arranged at the specialist children's unit, during which time, I was asked to present the case. The outcome was that he wasn't admitted and that he continued to progress: emotionally, academically and musically, both at school and at home. At home, he was no longer revered beyond his eight years and displaced. He had found the answer, but it wasn't Bio-active.

The next case, that of Adele, shows that she was similarly displaced and that she too had suffered rejection.

Chapter 8
Adele

It was an unusual beginning. I was working in a confidential drop-in centre for those under 25. There were no notes or referral information providing me with a history. Adele came into my consulting room, beaming. She appeared not to know how to start or what to say to me. She didn't give any indication of why she had come or what sort of trouble she was in. Neither was she distraught nor crying, so I let her lead the way.

Adele was excited to tell me that she had been adopted by a married couple in the UK. Her adoptive father was American, and her mother was English. They could not have children of their own, so they had chosen her. They then went to America as a family and lived there where Adele spent her early years. She had loved her father's American family and considered his extended family her own, integrating well. She recalled going to nursery school and then going to school in great detail, and she talked animatedly and affectionately of her cousins in America.

Her adoptive parents had divorced and Adele returned to England with her mother. She told me she missed her father, whom she loved very much, and his family. She presented differently in that she was always smiling and finished every sentence with "like that!". I spelt out what I could do, which was to work with her in a confidential manner, and that I would give her a hundred percent but that I would expect the same from her. I also explained that I would expect her to do homework. I placed emphasis on how we would both need to make a serious commitment and that she needed to consider carefully whether this was what she was willing to do. I offered her another appointment, interested to see if she would return and how the case would unravel. I really didn't know what the real purpose of her visit was and why she had decided to attend the drop-in centre, what was to most youngsters a last, desperate resort.

From what she had said, I suspected that she would have preferred staying in America than returning to the UK and the relative humdrum of a small county and living alone with her mother in very different and reduced circumstances. And that it was this sadness, that lay beneath her decision to attend the drop-in centre. Adele was experiencing what for anyone would be a very turbulent period, but it was particularly so for Adele, knowing this was the second time she had been rejected in her young life. But what I couldn't quite understand was her apparent mastery of her situation and lack of negativity and remorse. Like the agoraphobic hairdresser, she smiled all the time, relishing the opportunity to talk.

Adele arrived for the next appointment on time but limping. I asked her if she had been in the wars. She laughed and said she'd fallen off her bicycle in front of a bus – 'like that!'. She then explained in detail her visit to the local hospital: what the nurse had said, the local injection before the sutures, how the nurse had stitched the wound and the number of stitches. Then she related the detailed consequences: how she had to catch the bus instead of cycling everywhere. What was particularly alerting was how she appeared to relish relating the details and engaging with me. But at the same time, she was dismissive of the seriousness of the accident, making light of the danger to herself and to other people travelling in the bus. Noticeable also was that she said nothing about the pain or what might have been if the driver of the bus hadn't been vigilant. I was concerned particularly by the intricate story she was weaving, which had an almost seductive quality, ensnaring me with the intrigue of her life. I thought nothing more about the bus except that it was an accident.

On that second visit, she went on to describe her life in America and showed me photographs of 'her cousins in America', which she had brought with her. Noticeable was the degree to which she was explicit with details about the American family. She then told me, more as an incidental disclosure, about a 'friend' she had recently made in a local village and about his family, explaining how she would help his family by painting a fence and doing odd jobs around the home for them which they couldn't do for themselves. She explained that they couldn't write very well and that she would write letters for them – 'like that!'. Once again, the detail and the intensity with which she became involved was far from the usual teenage preoccupation. I was interested and alarmed that this so-called friend and his family appeared so dysfunctional and kept it on my radar. She hadn't yet disclosed what she needed to come for.

The next visit, Adele came in with an Elastoplast over her right eye. She engaged with me enthusiastically, once again, offering a detailed description of the hospital visit, including the nurse, the stitches, etc. I asked her if the nurse was the same one who had stitched her leg. No, Adele told me. It was a different hospital. I found that interesting. The following week, Adele attended with strapping on her wrist, and I realised the cuts were more than accidents. I had to assess what she would do if I confronted her in the present circumstances. I wondered if her visits to me were reinforcing her need to self-harm. Did she feel she had to interest me or impress me? With child self-referrals in particular, there is no referral information or recourse to a family doctor.

On the next occasion, Adele appeared with her hair cropped extremely short; although this in itself was not harmful, nevertheless, it was a cut. She had changed the strategy from falling off her cycle in public to harming herself in the privacy of her home. By this time, she had shown herself to be committed to her sessions with me. She was well organised, reasonable, respectful and punctual. But I realised she needed to receive the appropriate care and that the drop-in centre had no resources apart from the one-to-one confidential relationship. It was not set up to cope with the more serious disturbance manifested by Adele.

I confronted Adele with my concern for the mutilation, and she appeared to be relieved. I wanted her to agree that I should meet her adoptive mother in the first instance, and that secondly, I wanted her to see a psychiatrist. She agreed but wanted to continue visiting me. I told her I would need to discuss her continuing needs with whomever undertook her treatment and whatever was in her best interest, and this seemed to satisfy her. I didn't want her to feel another rejection because of me.

Her mother made an appointment to meet me. We met alone, with Adele waiting downstairs. Her mother appeared pleased and explained how she had had to return from the States, get a job and find a home for herself and Adele in much-reduced circumstances. I suspected that she was depressed and was struggling financially. Caught up in her own struggle, she hadn't become suspicious with the various cutting incidents, nor had she ever become involved with the hospital, for example, by accompanying Adele. However, she did know about the young man and his family, who she felt Adele had adopted. She said that she wasn't against Adele having friends, but this family bore no resemblance to her own relations and friends. I put it to her that I thought it was in Adele's best interest to refer her, and she readily agreed. She said that she perhaps had not been sufficiently aware of how the divorce had affected Adele, having been too preoccupied with how she would manage financially and with providing a home.

We invited Adele to join us, and her mother explained her own position and shortcomings. It went very well, and I saw this as a milestone, not for Adele to take on her mother's problems as well as her own, but at least, everything was out in the open. I wrote to the psychiatrist in the area explaining Adele's case, but he replied saying he did not treat personality disorders. Left with no alternative, I needed to dig deeper and confront Adele with her need to mutilate herself. She explained how she would get a razor blade, go in the bathroom, fill the bath, get in and then make an incision. As soon as she saw the blood appear, she would feel relief; she felt no pain. I told her firmly that if she cut herself anymore, I would cancel her next appointment. She never cut herself again. This may have seemed a drastic and perhaps un-therapeutic sanction, but I acted intuitively.

We had discussed her future together during our sessions, and she told me she wanted to enrol to take a nursing qualification and, eventually, work in an operating theatre. This sent alarm bells ringing. I could see Adele caring, but with her propensity for cutting, I felt this choice of career was inappropriate and not best suited to her needs. We explored other options. I asked her to visit the library as her homework and instructed her to come back with a list of career preferences. She was a bright girl, and with the relationship between her and her mother improving, I hoped that this difficult period they had both been through could be overcome. There was also talk of Adele visiting her father and his extended family in the States, which her mother encouraged. This demonstrated a certain generosity and understanding on the part of her mother. Adele stopped mutilating herself and was accepted for a course. The course work occupied and interested her, and I didn't see her again. I hoped that she would continue to improve.

Some two years later, I moved jobs to another hospital, and Adele managed to track me down. The hospital was in the countryside without a regular bus service, so I was very moved with her effort. She had come to show me her baby. I congratulated her on her lovely child, but inwardly, I felt misgivings. I promised to visit her when I could. I found her in a block of council flats. She had married the 'friend' and she was now pregnant with a second child. He was unemployed and had no positive features. Putting it mildly, she was 'nursing' him and his child. I was very sad because here was a lovely girl, bright and capable, saddled with a dysfunctional man without any prospects of improvement or a future. Adele, I knew, would have wanted what was best for her children, but in the circumstances, there would never be any chance of fulfilling this aim.

Looking back, Adele did not have the continuing support she needed. She lacked a family which would help her thrive, love her unconditionally, and with that love, provide discipline and caution her for her own protection. The case had come full circle. She was adopted. She then had to leave the family she loved in America, and now, she had created her own family. She had realised that dream, but at what cost?

Similarities in all of the case studies

The cost of the psychopathology in all of the cases that have been mentioned above was huge. The children were in danger of being misdiagnosed, labelled retarded, downgraded educationally and therefore, potentially, their whole future was put in jeopardy. They were usually just reacting to unbearable psychic pain caused by their families. The schools sometimes were found to collude with the families in condemnation of the children in a very sadistic and cruel manner. As a result, visiting the school and knowing what was happening in all sectors of the children's lives was vitally important. If I had just sat in my room with the children visiting me, I would never have been aware of what was happening to the children in their lives beyond, at school and at home. For this reason, I cannot understand the importance of play therapy or throwing paint on the walls. Relieving stress by this means is so transient; directly they return home, the situational causation is still there – not to mention the misplaced practice of throwing paint around. To a child, the message would be that you can throw paint. It was even encouraged. How inappropriate and confusing is that? Footwork is what is needed to become involved.

I tried to help and guide the children towards future goals, but inevitably, they or I would move away, and the thread of consistency would be broken.

The point I'd like to emphasise is this: with the exception of the children who referred themselves at the drop-in centre, even though it was the parents who caused the disorder, it was the named children who were the referred patients.

Chapter 9
The Power Behind Fragility

The referral came via the GP: A girl of 17, Lucy, had anorexia nervosa. Her weight was under seven stone and falling. As the consultant psychiatrist passed me the file, he said he was going on holiday and that he'd like her weight to improve before he returned. I didn't know why Lucy hadn't been referred before if she was so ill or why she wasn't in hospital. I suspected the family were resistant to outside intervention, as is often the case.

I rang the number on the referral letter and the mother answered. I introduced myself and asked her if I could make an appointment to see the family together. She seemed hesitant and nervous and became even more so when I asked if I could see the family preferably sitting together during my first visit. She said she'd see what she could do. I arrived at the address of a very nice house in a quiet village in Sussex. The mother answered the door and invited me in. She looked slightly unkempt, but her eyes said it all: worried and weary. As I entered the living room, first impressions were of a very disunited, anti-family group. The family consisted of three girls with ages from 17 to 21. The eldest was at college, the 19-year-old was at university and the youngest, Lucy, the patient, was attending school. All the girls were still living at home with their middle-aged parents.

In contrast with the mother, the rest of the family were acting in a very uncooperative, even rude, manner. The mother was clearly embarrassed by their behaviour. I introduced myself and suggested we sit round the table. They all showed their reluctance, moving to the table slowly and making noises to show how uncooperative they were. The intention was obvious: a united attempt to make me feel as uncomfortable as possible. I began by suggesting they introduce themselves and then asked for each family member to tell us their thoughts. The father began by saying he had better things to do with his time. This was followed by the two older girls agreeing with him. The mother was, by this time, crying and distraught: she disclosed how, despite her best endeavours to provide tasty food, the anorexic daughter, Lucy, just moved the food around on her plate with a fork and was still losing weight! Lucy sat hunched in a large jumper, hugging her knees, emaciated and detached, with a noticeable blue tinge round her lips. Nobody appeared to be concerned by Lucy's condition or by the outpouring and the obvious desperation and misery of the mother, who was left uncomforted and sobbing. They were dissociating themselves from the seriousness of the situation.

The older sister blurted out that she wanted to leave home as soon as she could and that she had had enough, her younger sister agreed. The older sister said she was fed up with sitting round the table for a meal and going through the same painful procedure having to witness Lucy rejecting food. She resented the time her mother spent shopping, cooking, worrying and pandering to Lucy. The mother interjected and asked what else could she do? See her daughter die from starvation? Lucy sat, seemingly impervious and unmoved by this outpouring. The second daughter said how they used to always enjoy mealtimes and that their mother was a very good cook, and now it was an experience that no one enjoyed. They were no longer a family. They would all prefer to go to McDonald's or get fish and chips and eat away from home.

Between the four walls of the house, there was a lot of suffering and I needed to locate the cause, however, time was not on my side. Clearly, Lucy was deteriorating rapidly.

I was pleased that I could experience the transference by feeling, hearing and witnessing the extent of the hostility and resentment towards me, but particularly towards the mother. They were all fed up with the control Lucy was exerting on the family; it had been going on for months. As I listened, I knew that they were right. It had gone on a long time – too long. This was a sick family. Although the resentment was centred around food, I knew this was not the real issue. My task was to bring about change to this much-disunited family as soon as possible. The only enduring relationship was built on the duty which existed between the mother and Lucy, but this was one-sided. I realised that this was the only opportunity I would have to see the family together again. So, I had to do something which would appeal to them all, but which included Lucy.

Treatment

When I had worked in the Misericordia hospital in Canada years previously, I had to give passive movements to two women who hadn't recovered from the anaesthetic during surgery. It was an odd experience: they were lying in private rooms intubated and unconscious, waiting to recover consciousness. I would quietly carry out the daily procedure of moving their joints in readiness for them, should they regain consciousness. I'd look at their faces and watch for them to frown, indicating that perhaps a joint might be stiff or painful, wondering what was going on and hoping they would recover. Sometimes, a nurse would come in and feed them via the tube. On one occasion, I asked her what they were fed with. She told me it was a particular product which contained everything necessary to keep them healthy: all the protein, minerals and vitamins they needed. And they did look healthy: their hair, nails and skin were obviously in a very good condition.

As I sat round the table amidst the hostility and looked at Lucy, I thought back to my experience in Canada. Lucy was too ill to engage in rational discussion and gaining her trust would have taken time which wasn't an option, considering the seriousness of her condition. I saw that the mealtimes were an essential part of the cohesiveness of the family and that since Lucy wasn't eating, she could be excused from mealtimes – providing that she drank the product I'd discovered in Canada. It was readily available in chemist shops, and I knew it would provide her with the nutrients she needed to keep her alive.

I addressed the mother with my proposal with the family listening: she was to stop her vigil in the kitchen and resume cooking for the family as she had done previously. I assured them all, the drink would provide Lucy with enough to sustain her. Lucy was reluctant, so I emphasised that seeing that she was still drinking, it would only take a minute to take the prescribed drink four times a day. The advantage to her was that she wouldn't have to struggle to eat at all. I needed to get them all to agree, including Lucy. The plan was for her mother to mix the drink and watch Lucy drink it. The family seemed to agree and approved the proposal, and I left, saying I would return.

The next day, I went to see the school where Lucy was studying for her A-levels. They were frightened by the seriousness and possible consequences of her condition. It was having a negative effect on the other children in Lucy's class. They were worried, in case the other children, acceptably boisterous at times, should knock into her. They too were going to extreme lengths to protect her and to ensure Lucy could sit the exams on time. She had stopped partaking in some classes and was provided with a taxi to school because she was so frail.

Two days later, I returned to see the mother alone; she appeared pleased to see me. I could see a slight change in her, and she reported that Lucy was drinking the nutriment drink, although reluctantly. She readily discussed the family and elaborated on Lucy's condition, which she told me, had deteriorated over a number of months. She explained that Lucy had been a Girl Guide and had been a Rover, participating in expeditions and camping, which she enjoyed. But she had given it up now because of her fragility; namely, because of the risk of permanent damage to her heart and bones which were affected by osteoporosis. She had developed downy hair all over her body, her periods had stopped four months previously, etc. The mother was pleased to tell me how the rest of the family were now sitting round the table and eating the meals she was preparing. On that occasion, I did not feel it appropriate to pry and ask her about her relationship with her husband. I just relied on her to tell me what she felt she wanted to.

I didn't know anything about causation, but several motives occurred to me. Could it be that Lucy was afraid of impending womanhood and university? Or was it the fear that this seemingly close-knit family appeared to be breaking up with the possibility of the older sisters moving away from home? I also knew Lucy's illness in itself would have affected the relationship between her parents. Was there any infidelity on the part of the father which Lucy had intuitively suspected thereby triggering the anorexia? Or was Lucy unconsciously trying to prevent them breaking up by uniting them with the concern of her illness?

I sensed the mother had indulged her family to her own detriment, so, I asked her about her own aspirations. She said she didn't have any – she was too busy with the family. I pointed out that she deserved more, that the girls would probably be leaving home and that she should look forward to her own future. I suggested she should go to the library and investigate possible careers and that we would discuss the options on my next visit. It was giving her permission to indulge in herself.

In the meantime, I was making progress with Lucy. Because she was better nourished, she was feeling better and did not look so transparent. I saw her condition as a symptom of turmoil and did not collude with the symptomatology of anorexia, such as discussing food or weighing her. What was now happening was a change in the family dynamics away from their preoccupation with cooking, shopping and miserable mealtimes. Lucy had now lost some of the control she had had. Previously, the family had gradually become involved in Lucy's illness, held to ransom and manipulated by her. Lucy needed to have the power she had exerted over the family taken from her. She had demonstrated that she couldn't survive if she continued. But neither could her family survive if the situation had been allowed to persist.

I revisited the school and gave the appropriate support to the staff, who were in a similar position to the mother, very fearful that Lucy might die.

The changes had to be almost imperceptible to Lucy, who had been in an exalted position. I did not want to progress too quickly so that she felt she was relinquishing the ground she had made and regret it by relapsing. It was a case of replacing the anorexia with achievements which ensured her future without her losing face.

The mother was relishing the prospects of a career, and her daughters were encouraging her to study for the exams which she would need if she were to become a teacher. When I called, and they were together, they laughed about their mother becoming a student, but they helped her with typing, applications and homework. They all saw the funny side and teased her, but they were also very respective and proud of her. She wanted, eventually, to study speech therapy. It was so good to see that she was earning the respect she deserved by all the family, including her husband.

Lucy was obviously better, but at no time did I feel it appropriate to weigh her. Nevertheless, I did wonder what her weight was.

The GP was kept informed by letter, and he decided to ask her to 'jump on the scales'. She had put on two kilos. She took her exams and passed well, and we continued to meet and discuss how she felt about everything, including boyfriends and the future. She was now allowed to sit round the table with the family as long as she ate. With support, she gradually improved and didn't relapse, which I was afraid was a possibility, given the antecedents of the case.

Postscript

Two years later, I was travelling on a train to London; walking through the carriage was Lucy's mother. She spotted me, but I didn't recognise her – she looked radiant! She asked me if she could blow her own trumpet. She told me she was on her way to an interview as a speech therapist. Lucy was at university.

A biopsychosocial approach

As a therapist, but new to family therapy, this was my first case involving anorexia. I did not view it – perhaps naively – any differently to any other referred case. Key to my involvement was intuition, feeling, witnessing and thinking it through on that first visit, seeing where the power lay. Where my involvement did differ was in the recognition that Lucy's condition was both physical and mental, and, as I explained, I did not have time on my side. In this case, the family behaviour and that of the school had become entrenched and was leading to rapid deterioration. The situation needed to be radical and managed. To put a grand title on my intervention, it was a biopsychosocial approach. My experience as a mother, as a physical therapist and then as a family therapist quite naturally suggested to me that if my patients had maybe a drug- or drink-related or, in this case, eating disorder, my first thought should be to question whether they were in sufficient health to concentrate and engage with what I had to offer. The immediate need was to save Lucy's life. She needed nutriments. My only resource was myself. Hence my biopsychosocial approach.

My concern was for the whole family. The assumption was that they were all under-functioning and miserable. This was serious, particularly as the individual futures of all the girls and the choices they made may have been influenced by the circumstances they were now caught up in. My treatment strategy, in general, relied on assessing each case differently and formulating a strategy to change the family dynamics. Underlying this particular case was the power Lucy exerted by exercising the ultimate outcome: death. I needed to take away that power from Lucy and then, gradually, relinquish it from me back to the family, to the school and to Lucy. The school and family, from being impotent and colluding in the psychopathology, needed to learn. It was an education for the school staff. To their credit, they embraced the situation and came up trumps, as did the family.

Death was the threat which frightened everyone in Lucy's case. She was blackmailing her family and her school. In the next case, there was no blackmail. The psychopathology was accepted by everyone – even the patient, Fergus – as permanent. But patients all hold the ultimate power to live or give up.

Chapter 10
Fergus

For therapists, every new patient is an encounter, a journey tinged with excitement, responsibility and privilege but also risks. In this case study, the outcome was sad and unexpected and left me recalling not only the beginning and the end of the journey, but also what happened in between. But of course, it wasn't the end; the end is what we learn and take to heart – a legacy. I can reproach myself for not doing more, but I was only reaching out to those chronic cases because no one else was doing anything proactive for them.

The local paper had a section concerned with petty crime, and very occasionally, I would glimpse through and read colourful reports of court appearances. Some became familiar just because the name kept reappearing. One such name was Fergus O Donovan. He was infamous locally, and his lawyer defended him loyally year by year. The police appeared to view him with a degree of acceptance, taking his offences for granted. The offence was always drink-related. I have to claim that I pictured him as a burly Irishman, strong, aggressive, brutal and frightening when under the influence. So, this was the background to my first encounter with Fergus.

In person, I first met him in a bed of newly planted wallflowers outside the window of the boardroom at the asylum where I worked. On that morning, I was running a course titled 'The Containment of Violent Patients'. The asylum boardroom was where the course was being held. The lecturer was doing his stuff at the blackboard and everything was set for the course attendees to return to their respective hospitals more confident that they could contain difficult patients in the most effective and efficient manner. The need had arisen in this and other asylums because the historical use of strait jackets and padded cells, for the purpose of restraint and containment, were no longer available. A new regime and breed of staff had to deal with such patients without these adjuncts to treatment, hence the course.

Listening to the lecture, I became aware of a face in cuffed hands pressed against the window. It wasn't a particularly attractive face! It was framed with greasy, black hair, had a florid complexion, with eyes peering through dirty horn-rimmed spectacles into the boardroom. Sensing disruption and not wanting to disturb the class from their instruction, I quickly made my way from the room, past reception and outside. In the flowerbed, the figure was still peering in through the window. Very stealthily, I joined the figure, tiptoeing in the flowerbed so as not to crush the wallflowers, and gently took his elbow. He turned around and smiled at me. I took his arm and led him away from the window and asked his name. "Fergus," he said. "Fergus O Donovan."

Was this really the notorious drunk whom I had imagined as frightening? He asked me who I was, and when I told him my name, he slurred, "Wait." He then fished around in his jacket pocket, swaying and lurching. I needed to hold him to steady him and prevent him from falling. Eventually, he retrieved a tiny, rather dirty square of paper. To my amazement, it was a paper I had written on stress and personality a few years earlier (Thomson, nee Evans, 1980)! Incredulous at this coincidence, I wanted to know more. But I couldn't spend more time with Fergus and ponder over the meeting and how he had managed to obtain a copy of my research. Nevertheless, it was and still is an incredible encounter and coincidence! As far as I knew, nobody in the asylum was interested in this research.

As amazing as this first encounter was, it was now my duty to return to the class, ensuring the course members had their coffee break, being available to answer questions and generally being on hand.

That meeting with Fergus was just the beginning. I can't remember how, but he became a member of a group I was running, attached to my job as deputy manager of the asylum. The members of the group that had been referred to me for rehabilitation were best described by the word 'eclectic'. However, the word eclectic was stretched, to say the least. Most of them were chronic drug users or alcoholics who had no expectation of a change of circumstances; they were entrenched in the subculture of abuse.

The day started with coffee, after which the group members did jobs round the hospital, such as washing cars (for which we charged), or they helped in the wards, or sweeping up leaves, etc. As a group, they met for lunch and then again for group therapy with me over tea, after which, they left for home, wherever that happened to be, to return the next day. Any money we raised, I would use to fund someone willing to come and teach some skill or pastime to the group. An artist came on Wednesdays, and they all did drawing. A lady came with her knitting machine, and some of them made scarves. While they were busy, I was trying to ensure the hospital was ticking over.

My aim was to help them abstain whilst establishing a pattern and purpose in their lives that would prepare them for work and freedom from the hold the substance had over them. I had no involvement with their prescribed drugs and treatment. The group became friends and would help each other with advice to ride the ups and downs of life (for them, there had been many more downs than ups). Sustaining them and demonstrating their self-belief, nurturing their talents and aspirations was working well within the group.

Diagnostically, they were suffering from personality disorders: to me, they all had stories which had set them on the wrong path, which they could not quit. They were caught in currents without any control, floundering hopelessly towards rapids and clinging on to whatever they could to keep them in touch with reality. They were self-treating with whatever they could lay their hands on to blur that reality. They had all spent time in the asylum as patients, been in prison or were involved with the judiciary. Fergus became a member following that first encounter. They became as near to a family as they could, empathising with each other's predicaments, happy when they had survived a weekend without drugs or drink and welcoming Mondays and the safe ritual it heralded for the coming week.

The group was self-funding, inconspicuous to the hospital as a whole, nameless, yet dependent and attached to the asylum without resources: eating its food, occupying a spare disused flat and a small kitchen. They were not depressed: life for them was about comparisons – compared with the life that had gone before, this was much better, and they were proud of their achievements, however small. They were developing identities, savouring the experiences they had never had, discovering taste, smell and an appreciation of beauty previously denied to them, and experiencing what it was like to be a child, as if for the first time. They were changing – emerging like chrysalises into characters, establishing identities, discovering themselves. Interestingly, they would confess that they were genuinely frightened because they did not know who or what they were without the influence of alcohol or drugs. Their development had been arrested sometimes from a very early age.

On a Friday afternoon, I would ask them to prepare for the weekend, the worse time for them. Washing clothes was now something they needed to do. Charity shops would provide them with clothes, but naturally, the clothes needed laundering – something which hadn't concerned some of them before. Fergus would explain how he planned to cut the grass at the Roman Catholic Church on Saturday morning, followed by the grass at the Church of England graveyard in the afternoon. Then, he quite liked going to the laundrette on Sunday morning to launder his bed linen and to get his clothes ready for the next week. He enjoyed seeing the washing go around. Fergus, in the past, had had no home; he would sleep on tombstones in the cemetery. Conveniently, across the road was a shop that opened early where he could buy alcohol. He would tell the group how he would wake to find rats gnawing at his shoe leather in the winter when they were hungry.

For Sundays, I encouraged them to use their bus passes to go on trips and take a packed lunch. This was the one concession the hospital allowed – a bus pass. It owed this concession to the blind-eyed approach of one particular woman. I had a few of these important individuals who would favour me with various resources, which made such a difference to what I could do wearing my therapist cap, without incurring budgetary difficulties wearing my manager's hat.

On one occasion, newly in post, I was left in charge of the now closed Sussex asylum. All hell broke loose. The temperature dropped and it snowed. The ceilings in the wards leaked, nurses couldn't get into work, a patient started punching nurses, and, to cap it all, a patient absconded. There were no contingency plans, but the patient, a lady, had to be found. She had escaped during the night in just a nightdress, unnoticed by the night staff. We turned the boardroom into an operations room. A map of the area was put on the blackboard, and search teams were organised to scan the area. The police, the fire service, the radio hams, air search and rescue – all descended on the hospital purported to be haunted. My patient group were put in charge of caring for these various emergency personnel. Fergus took to wheeling a trolley with tea, sandwiches and cakes. He took great pleasure in speaking to the police force, who all knew him so well over the years as a notorious drunk in the cells.

The police inspector said, "Fergus? I'm dumbfounded! I've only ever seen you drunk!"

"Oh yes, Inspector, this is how it's done!" and Fergus poured tea with some delicacy and aplomb. "Can I offer you a cheese scone, sir…? Oh, Sergeant, I see your cup is empty, and I know you take one sugar and you like strong tea."

"Fergus, I can't believe it. I never thought I'd see you looking after me," a sergeant replied.

The police were incredulous at the change in him and at the progress he had made. They similarly saw old acquaintances amongst the group who had been in court for various offences.

Sad as it was for the poor lost patient, the group benefitted from being in a position of serving and earning respect by those very people they had come to dislike and fear. (The lost patient amazingly was found alive after four days.) My fear was of how much this would affect the hospital budget, but amazingly, no service claimed expenses.

The group and Fergus were doing well, and I began to discuss with them a future with paid employment. We had ups and downs, but they needed to learn to ride these and survive. They were now doing night classes and tentatively exploring relationships beyond the group. Socialising was an important step for them; previously, socialising was restricted to a peer group of similar abusers. Writing their own stories was added to the list of things to do, helped by a poet who was interested in contributing. Fergus was becoming very expressive, writing a daily diary and exploring literature. I was hopeful that he could develop this aptitude for expression and perhaps take a course leading to a degree.

But it wasn't to be! One Monday morning, I had a phone call from the superintendent of police who said, "I've got some very bad news for you. Fergus is dead."

I went to the funeral and was among a huge congregation of police, shopkeepers, 'off-licensers' and churchgoers from two churches – it was packed. After asking around, I eventually met the only member of his family to attend – a sister from Ireland – to see if I could comfort her. She seemed bemused.

Fergus had left a legacy: there were many unanswered questions. *Why did he die? What had happened?* I even wondered if I had inadvertently played a part in his premature death by somehow pitching his future too high. One of the tasks I had required of the group was to write their stories. Before his death, Fergus had written his story and had given it to me. It's a story without an ending, like those of so many of our patients in similar situations. Sometime later, the police from the main police station sent me two photos they had taken of Fergus. They too were left grieving like me and wondering what might have been.

A legacy

So, what was Fergus's legacy to me as a therapist? First, was my being negatively influenced by the local paper and then putting my own spin on someone I had never met. Second, there was the coincidence: Fergus getting my research and knowing my name. Fergus didn't even read the local paper, never mind a research report. I never did ask him how he came to know me via my research before that first meeting in the flowerbed. In retrospect, of course, I wish I had. I can only say that I was extraordinarily busy and knew that all in good time, further down the line, that question would be answered. Furthermore, Fergus was not the only patient; they were all vulnerable, trying to find themselves. The dynamic between them was interdependent and critical, and I couldn't favour just one.

Third, the benevolence of the police was wonderful to observe. They'd had years of Fergus in the cells, seeing him at his worst, putting up with his behaviour, feeding him, giving him tea and much more. They were police officers and interested in improvement, but they were helpless to intervene therapeutically. They were incredulous when they saw the tables turned in the boardroom, realising that Fergus was looking after them, and how proud they were to be witnessing this profound change.

Some will miss the point and view Fergus quite wrongly as a criminal. What I'm keen to convey is that, as therapists, we need to realise therapy is a two-way process. We need to be professional and knowledgeable. We also need to be passionate and genuinely intrigued by our patients, delving into the past, identifying where things went wrong, listening to their stories. If we can demonstrate and impart our intentions for them, they will appreciate the understanding and the trust they crave, and the motivation to change will follow.

And last, there was the funeral. The church had been packed with people coming to pay their respects and to say goodbye to a notorious and once-broken man, but a man who had clearly touched their hearts. How was it that they all came together at such a short notice? He didn't even belong or attend a church. What did I learn and take away from this brief encounter that began in the emerging wallflower-bed and ended with mountains of flowers fully blooming on Fergus's simple pauper's coffin? (The police sent me photos of Fergus they had taken, which, of course, I've still got.) I learned that the last becomes first.

Chapter 11
Sonya: Lame Dog and Beyond! A Family Therapy Case Study

The referral came via the GP: a girl of ten was suffering from encopresis. I made an appointment to visit the family with some urgency. The family lived on the outskirts of town in a Victorian semi-detached house. When I arrived, it was a desperate scene: Joan, a young woman, was pregnant and trying to cope with a crying child hanging onto her skirt. She was alone with the child, and my request for a meeting with all the family present was obviously not going to happen. Joan told me the family consisted of the toddler and three children of school age. The little girl with encopresis, Sonya, was the eldest of the children now at school. Joan's partner was the father of the children, including the unborn child. The father was away all the week, and sometimes much longer, working as a shop fitter.

The young woman looked depressed and downtrodden. She just couldn't cope. Joan cried while explaining the position. She had been a student nurse, aged 20, enjoying her training, when she met John, aged 45. John was divorced. His previous wife had left him in the house with the four children. Joan and John started a relationship. Joan became pregnant and then moved into the home with John and his four children. John then took a job away in another part of the country, which meant he was away for increasingly long lengths of time, leaving Joan alone to look after his children.

The children were insecure. They had lost their own mother, who now had nothing to do with them. Money was tight and Joan didn't have enough to manage. On top of this, Sonya began soiling and smearing, which involved all the extra work: washing, drying, wiping the mess off the walls and dealing with the smell. It was not surprising that Joan was depressed. She felt John was taking advantage of her. She told me that she wanted to turn back the clock and continue training for the profession she loved. She knew she had made a huge mistake. She told me she disliked Sonya because of the soiling and explained how Sonya would soil her underwear and then hide it in a drawer, which would then contaminate and soil the clean clothes in the drawer. Sonya would also smear faeces all over the bedroom, which meant the house always smelt, but it was very difficult to clean. No sooner had Joan cleaned, then Sonya would repeat the soiling. Joan couldn't keep up with the relentless demands of Sonya's soiling and looking after the children. John, the children's father, would only come home briefly and then leave again, unconcerned about Joan, the children and the mess he was leaving behind. Joan sobbed, explaining that she couldn't go on. I left her, realising that the situation was critical.

Joan was now the pivot of the family, albeit a reluctant one. I could see that she was, in fact, a very good, caring young woman, who couldn't just up sticks and leave the children to the mercy of their father, although that was clearly what she most wanted to do.

My next task was to visit Sonya's school. I arranged to see the headmaster and find out how Sonya was managing but also to see how the other two children were reacting. The headmaster was very welcoming and proud of his school. Sonya, he told me, was a very good pupil, but the staff had noticed deterioration recently: she appeared ill and they didn't know why. They did not report that she was soiling at school, which was interesting. They said that she would 'mother' her brother and sister and was an influence for good on the other children in the classroom. I didn't disclose the whole story but explained to the staff that Sonya was a very disturbed little girl and asked them for their help and forbearance while I was trying to help the family. They were very understanding and cooperative. I left them, suggesting I would return in due course. Various social workers had been involved but hadn't visited recently. If they had, they would have most probably put the children into care.

Time was not on my side. The problem had not occurred overnight but over a number of months. Clearly, it was a family problem. On the one hand, I needed to support Joan; on the other, I needed to help Sonya. I arranged to meet Sonya on her own. She was a frail, slight, nervy child, fidgeting with her clothes and staring, preoccupied, out the window. I started gently trying to engage with her, and eventually, she turned to look at me and told me about school that day. I felt I had made a good start, and together, we joined Joan in the living room to have a cup of tea. Joan talked about her nurse training and what she liked about it, and Sonya appeared interested.

I could see that they both had loss in common: Joan, a loss of freedom and Sonya, a loss of her mother and stability. I knew Sonya was responsible enough to also have worried about her brother and sisters. When Joan and Sonya were together, there was no obvious animosity between them. If I could strengthen their relationship, then there might be hope of stopping the soiling, thus reducing the burden Joan was carrying, and maybe they would help one another. They both had the quality of caring and kindliness.

I decided that I would aim to take them out together, away from the home, while the youngest toddler was at nursery. It was a very successful but simple outing, just looking at clothes in the shops walking round the cathedral grounds and ending up with tea and cake in a little restaurant. They chatted together throughout, and I could see a relationship in the making. They had a lot in common. I repeated the outings regularly, leaving them with little tasks they could share, such as sewing, etc.

But I needed to speak to the father. It sensed he was avoiding me and I hadn't yet met him. Two months after the first meeting with Joan, I met him. He wasn't impressive. He wasn't prepared to do anything and didn't show any responsibility towards his family at all. It was obvious he was using his job as an excuse to stay away. He tried flattering me – obviously, used to conning his way through life. I also met the remainder of the children who were all suffering in different ways – in this respect, the school staff were amazing, thinking up different ways of intervening such as awarding gold stars to the children and particularly selecting the children for different school involvements to raise their self-esteem. I continued to influence the relationship between Joan and Sonya in various ways.

The breakthrough came when Joan rang me because she was excited to tell me that Sonya had won an award and she was so pleased. Joan and Sonya were sharing household jobs, shopping and jokes. Sonya had stopped soiling and smearing. Joan had the baby, which was swiftly followed by the bank foreclosure on the house: the father had not been making mortgage payments. The family were rehoused into local authority housing. Social services called an 'at risk meeting', and the chief social worker asked why the family had received so little support and why it had all been left to me, a family therapist. Social services took over from me, providing resources for the family which I did not have access to.

Sometime later, Joan came to see me, saying she was pregnant again and she wanted advice; she was thinking of a termination. We caught up on the family situation, and I was pleased to hear that both Sonya and Joan were getting on well and that Sonya was doing well at a new school. We parted with Joan needing to decide about the unborn child. Some months later, Joan again asked to see me and showed off a new-born baby. She told me that the money which was returned to them, once the house was sold by the bank, was being spent on a wonderful Christmas. Lavish presents were bought for the children, including drum kits for the boys (in a small terraced house?), party frocks, etc., for the girls. And a family dog had been rescued from a dog shelter. The dog had a deformity which would cost £3,000 in vet bills! Various images passed through my mind: How would the very near neighbours react to two sets of drum kits? And why on earth select a deformed dog?

Postscript

Some years later, I was delighted to see Sonya as the subject of an editorial! Social services were writing in the local paper about their success stories. She was obviously doing well: the picture showed her looking very attractive and living in a nice house. She was married with two children of her own. She had a baby on her knee and the other child, a toddler, was cuddling the baby.

Chapter 12

Magic Mushrooms to a Midas Moment: William's Journey

"Can you see a young man now?" the receptionist queried.

"Yes, send him up please," I replied.

I waited to hear his footsteps coming up the stairs. I was always aware of the desperation behind taking such a big step for young people – to come to a drop-in centre alone, especially if they were in danger of being followed by drug pushers or if they had broken the law. They were vigilant, anxious and streetwise.

He hesitated outside my small consulting room before bursting in. His appearance suggested his circumstances: he looked menacing, with tussled ginger hair, a florid, unshaven face, dilated pupils, unkempt – and defensive maybe?

I stood up to welcome him and offered to shake his hand.

"I want to get off drugs," he said, coming straight to the point.

"Well, come and sit down," I offered. "Would you like a cup of tea?"

He blinked, somewhat surprised, and said yes.

I came back with the tea, and as he sipped it, he looked at me, apparently assessing me and obviously needing some assurance that he had come to the right place. However, more importantly, he needed to know that I could withstand and deliver what he wanted.

"I've fractured a man's skull," he volunteered. "And broken another's arm."

"Are you perhaps testing me out?" I ventured. "Seeing whether I can withstand you and help you?"

He was pleased with my reply. We both smiled knowingly.

He was in poor shape: lice were on his clothing, and he looked unhealthy. He appeared to be 19 or 20 and was of moderate height.

In such cases, I followed my well-trodden formulae: I would lay out what I could do and what they would need to do and suggested that they go away and consider if they were willing to commit and give a hundred percent. If they were, I'd match it.

I would then assess how compromised the patient was health-wise, questioning if they were eating anything in the way of nutrition, and if not, I would instruct them to buy a packet of muesli and a pint of milk. If they had no money, I'd give them enough to purchase it. It was pointless to begin a therapeutic relationship if the patient was mentally and physically compromised and undernourished.

I'd then explain the contract: It would be the most difficult undertaking that they would ever have to participate in. However, it would also be the most incredible journey of discovery (Later, I would come to regret not taking photographs at initial meetings to compare them with their discharge in the months ahead. However, such an action would be prohibitive in the circumstances). I would assure them what the sessions would consist of. I would stress this commitment and not send them away under the impression that I was the main player but that they were. Thus, it was reversing the usual expectations of patients and the attitude of the National Health Service (NHS), which was that the patients become passive recipients of finances, treatment and social support. This approach was adopted to act as a deterrent; I had not the time or resources for them to be passive recipients.

William returned and began to tell his story. In William's case, his father had been awarded custody by the courts. His mother left, and his father remarried, and William lived with his father and his new wife. The new wife neglected him because she didn't want the responsibility of someone else's child. He started school, but because his mother didn't get up in the morning, he was always late and was consequently punished and made to stand outside the classroom. As a family therapist, I was appalled by the apparent lack of understanding on the part of the teachers. Children living in such turmoil would look ill, unhealthy, uncared for and unloved. They would often be hyperactive or the class clown, covering the substitute depressive illness. The teachers seldom appreciated these children as ill or as victims. William described how he felt after the divorce.

When his mother left, he did not understand and remembered feeling guilty. He became labelled a 'naughty child' both at school and at home.

Children experiencing the same persecution would find a natural affinity for each other. They found magic mushrooms instantly took effect and made them feel better. They would progress up the ladder to any form of mood-altering substance (i.e. sniffing glue or drinking alcohol). Feeling like outcasts, they started missing school. Their only aim was to feel better whatever the cost. Some would steal to fuel the increasingly addictive habit. They would, as they became more desperate, pick out children at school who looked unhappy and vulnerable and offer them drugs. They knew that these children were potential drug addicts like themselves who would in turn finance their increasing need for drugs.

I asked William about his birth mother. William felt she must have blamed him for the divorce and that she did not love him. He had not seen her since she left the home when he was five. His education was non-existent; his only support and sense of belonging came from his substitute family – the other children in similar circumstances. He told me that apart from working harder and harder to fuel his increasing addiction, he did like drawing.

The present

William was bright and well-motivated, but he needed to understand that his childhood had been skewed and that in no way could he be blamed for his parents' divorce. His childhood had not prepared him for a life free from drugs. Everything revolved around and was influenced by drugs: his work that he needed in order to finance the habit, the friends he had, the lack of security. He had not developed mentally, and returning to live in a society that had ostracised him was a far cry from life in the skewed society where he felt he belonged.

I had no resources to use to help him and the others like him. I had no hospital bed where he could be safely weaned off the drugs. For these patients, it was cold turkey unless they wanted to be referred, which they seldom did. I had no prescription pad. I did have people I knew whom I could tap for certain types of help, but this help was limited. Together, we only had our joint will to succeed. I never concentrated on drug withdrawal, although we discussed how this could be achieved. We concentrated on the excitement of discovering who he was and his own potential. As strange as it may seem, this aspect of giving up addiction was the most frightening for them. Some would own that they might be monsters.

Over the weeks, we began to unravel what had led to his present predicament and what lay ahead if he was able to become drug and alcohol-free. No doubt, sometimes he must have felt that the demands on him were too great and that it would be easier to revert to his old ways. This was a very lonely and vulnerable period.

These patients were wary of the drug pushers who had been supplying their habit to various extents. Some had pushed drugs themselves, so they knew the score. The penalty for anyone breaking ranks was a bullet in the knee joint. Even attending the drop-in centre was precarious. However, William was not scared. He had had a terrible life and was used to fighting and looking after himself. He even appeared to enjoy the challenge. What Rutter (1999) called steeling or resilience came into play.

The future

The main challenge was to prepare William in a developmental sense to make the future better, to help him discover some new horizon that was both achievable and exciting. As a therapist, I was always assessing what I had to work with, much like a sculptor. Although William had had no education, I could see how bright he was. One day, he brought in a beautiful drawing of a tiger that had not been copied but designed by him. With all my patients, I would ask them what their pipe dream was, and I was not surprised to learn that William's dream was to be a designer or an artist. I could see that his dream was a realistic goal. By attending night school, he could develop along with others with similar aims and enjoy and tolerate the new experience. I say tolerate because his/their world was so much tougher than society in general. I needed to ensure that they would look and behave appropriately and not blot their copybooks. They needed to be acceptable.

After about four months, William had changed beyond recognition. He was off drugs and doing very well. During one session, I decided to broach the subject of his mother. Previously,

I had sensed it was too sensitive an issue for him to discuss. However, now with William sitting in front of me, clean and proud of what he'd achieved, I felt I could ask him how he felt towards her.

"She couldn't love me, could she?" he asked. We talked about what his mother might feel, about the possibility that she might feel guilty for leaving him, which was something he had never considered. The conversation turned to where she was. He thought he knew where she worked. I seized the opportunity and offered to telephone her there and then. He was very uneasy and obviously perturbed. However, after giving it some thought, he said, "Give it a go." I rang the number and as it happened, his mother took the call. I introduced myself and then told her that I had William with me.

"Where are you?" she said. "I'm at work, but I'm coming right now."

We waited nervously while she travelled from a nearby town.

They met not with laughter but with tears, sobbing in each other's arms. That is what he needed – what they both needed. The question of love came up, and she told him that not a day had passed when she had not thought about him. She explained that she had not wanted to unsettle him by contacting him and that she thought he wanted to be with his father!

If she had known what he had endured to reach this point, she would have been rightly perturbed, but now she could be proud of her son.

Postscript

William was on his way to fulfilling his pipe dream, and I discharged him. He presented me with a beautiful painting.

However, that was not the end. Later, when I worked in a psychiatric hospital, he tracked me down. I was thrilled to see him. I appreciated the effort involved and asked him if he would like a cup of tea and chat. While we were catching up and sipping tea, he placed £250 on the table, "This is for you to help someone like me." I looked at him. Nobody would ever realise the path he had trod and the journey we had taken together. I was so proud and privileged to have been part of that journey of discovery.

The survival of children such as William, unloved and even hated at the age of five and left to themselves, is cruelty in the extreme. I don't feel they can ever truly heal. Every aspect of their future is jeopardised. And yet, society is causing this deprivation. Family breakdown is rife, and new wives, husbands or partners can resent or detest the children they have inherited.

Teachers really do need, at the very least, to be educated if they have not the empathy, insight and love to realise these children are in desperate need to be understood, not punished.

I've tried to explain and make the case that people are systems made up of networks and associations which include teachers, schools and all the influences of which these various but interrelated parts are composed. The mind and body should not be divided, nor should treatment be devoted to one without acknowledging the consequences to the other. The next chapter makes the point that even pets are pertinent and sometimes pivotal to treatment.

Chapter 13
Significant Others

In writing this book as a therapist, I am concerned with symptoms of distress which amount to and contribute to the formulation of diagnostic criteria. The focus in this chapter is on patients and their pets from two patient settings: the family therapy unit and the adult general psychiatric service. Within the family therapy unit, we were concerned with children with two diagnostic criteria: either an emotional or a conduct disorder. With the adults, we were concerned with general diagnostic criteria associated with psychiatry.

As a family therapist who was visiting families in their homes, I discovered that some homes and circumstances were more unusual than others. But whatever the circumstances, I have learnt that all information is relevant, only differing in degrees of relevance. Whether it was the extended family, the neighbours, the living amenities, debts, illness or skeletons in the cupboards – all provided the background narrative enabling me to understand the family dynamics and helping to formulate where the causative bottlenecks were and to assess what form my intervention would take. I liken this to getting on the wavelength of the patients.

In family therapy, the children were always the reason for the referral. But invariably, the children were only reacting to problems within the family and were caught up in dynamics which they did not understand. So often, they were made the scapegoats, as previous case studies have illustrated. Their referral reactions were associated with hyperactivity, disruption, stealing, night terror, failure to develop normal milestones, enuresis, encopresis or the symptoms of disturbance. Often, if they were of school age, the school dealt with them as 'naughty' and they were punished. The family would, in the extreme cases, ask for them to be removed from the home, believing that the family would settle down and be better off without them. Often, the school and the family ganged up on the children in an attempt to justify the 'punishment' of the children.

In general psychiatry, it was a different story. Patients were often feeling alone and alienated, struggling to work out why they were ill, where they had gone wrong or who or what circumstances they could blame. Some would hang on to the past, unable to view a future, remaining in ditches they had dug for themselves, too fearful or perhaps even too comfortable to get out. Once a diagnosis was made, the treatment resources were rolled out. However, they too may well have been children who were themselves victims of childhood trauma, as seen in the family therapy service.

What may appear to be a light-hearted chapter is not just about the patients, but about the patients with their pets, the pets I encountered as a therapist whilst visiting these families in their homes. To put this chapter in perspective, it was developed as a result of an invitation by a journal to submit 'a manuscript'. This submission led to others in which I have presented case studies, each one concentrating on a particular family. This invitation was a departure from my more usual research manuscripts, but it did strike a chord, confronting the objective versus subjective personal encounter, which propelled me into thoughts resulting from my therapeutic experience and my experience as a research scientist. I found that on the one hand, research was objective, but my subjective thoughts and experiences were building and fuelling a foundation from which I formulated the research hypotheses which I then tested. I could not do either justice without the other.

My first departure from research was a manuscript designed to get feedback from therapists: 'Manikins, Nursery Rhymes and Secrets' (discussed above). I really didn't know if I was the only therapist to identify a mechanism in which the children who had been referred to the family therapy unit were, via manikins, nursery rhymes and secrets, conveying the source of their psychic pain.

When I made the connection myself, I was elated, and that is not an exaggeration. It enabled me to short-circuit the therapeutic process. I understood the sadness and the loneliness these children were experiencing with no means to convey their impossible plight, the injustice and the consequences. The objects they identified with, whether rings, books, manikins, etc., encapsulated their difficulties in one, as it were!

This chapter, therefore, follows in a similar vein, asking why do these families have unusual pets. What does it say, if anything, about the psychopathology? Eysenck (1967) and Glezer, Felthous and Holzer (2002) both made the connection that cruelty and psychopathology are correlated, but neither went as far as to say this involved 'unusual pets'. Begging the question, can I expect unusual pets in families experiencing distress? Similarly, can I expect and should I listen and look for the symbols used to conceptualise disorder? Should I perhaps test the hypotheses?

I said at the beginning that this chapter may appear 'light-hearted', but these encounters were strange, even amusing and intriguing; however, they were sometimes far from light-hearted, having even sinister and serious implications. Strange as it may seem, the pets became part of the family dynamics and were often central to the various strategies these troubled families employed. So powerful were the influence of some pets, that the serious decision of a divorce, for example, with its huge consequences involving children, finance, selling the home, etc., were deferred because of the love of a dog.

Eysenck (1967) in describing the characteristics of high-scoring psychoticism patients, explains that socialisation is particularly alien to them, describing them as odd, isolated, troublesome, lacking in human feelings for fellow human beings and for animals. He explains that such 'children' try to make up for lack of feeling by indulging in sensation-seeking 'arousal jags'.

When it comes to my curiosity about families and pets, I suspect that I am not alone and that these tales will provoke many a memory in therapists with similar backgrounds. Like me, they may well have become intrigued by the relationship between patients and their pets. But to therapists newly embarking on a career, it is an interesting but neglected topic/observation and one which I hope will interest those who read this book. I have found that the more I make connections, the more interesting, exciting and effective my intervention becomes.

The first example begins with Bruce, a stray dog with a really empathic nature. What became of him, I do not know, but I still feel for his welfare, for, as I explain, he became part of my patch.

Bruce

Bruce was a mongrel dog rescued by an alcoholic couple during one of their many periods of sobriety and during one of their attempts to stop drinking. Bruce appeared to be the addition to the family that they never had. The couple, Cora and Scott, were childless, unemployed and living on benefits in social housing. They were, when sober, full of regrets for their misspent lives and keen to reform. They would try to impress with their intent to become good, responsible citizens – 'this time'. Prior to Bruce, their lives would be a revolving door of being on drink, then off drink, being penitent, trying to reform in hospital and coming out of hospital. Then Cora would steal drink from a shop, ensuring she was seen on the CCTV cameras. She would return to prison where she enjoyed 'trusty' status and where she felt secure.

Prison was the only place where she was away from temptation, where she had respect and status. In prison, she was reliable, caring, respected and motherly towards the younger women offenders. The staff were always welcoming; after all, I suppose she made their lives easier. Cora and Scott started drinking to obliterate painful memories associated with abuse during their childhoods. Like many patients, they had an affinity with each other through their shared experience of abuse. Patients of abuse at the hands of others can use personal abuse as an excuse to take no responsibility for themselves in the present.

Cora's partner, Scott, was also an alcoholic, and synchronising the abstaining periods when they were both intent on abstinence was predictably hazardous. It was always the aim to ensure that they could support one another, but inevitably, the difficulty and pressure of living drink-free was too much, and when one started drinking, the other would soon follow. Apart from being born in Scotland, a history of drinking, theft, abstinence, hospitalisation, then failure and prison, the alcoholic problem was the only behaviour they had in common.

They were a likeable couple who would attend the alcohol group we ran, full of support and kindness towards the other alcoholics who, like them, were trying to give up drinking. This group, apart from the psychotherapy, would exchange stories of their lives as an alcoholic; for example, when they were drinking, they shared the same problems of where to get rid of the empty bottles. Cora and Scott would explain how they managed: they had the strategy of walking into town such that they passed many litterbins, and into these, they would feed the empty bottles, two at a time. By the time they reached the supermarket, they had dispensed with all the empty bottles, and they could restock with more alcohol and return home. Other members of the group would share how they dispensed with empty bottles by hiding them in the sleeves of clothes hanging in a wardrobe or placing them on beams in a garage. All these strategies were aimed at hiding the evidence but carried the additional burden that, one day, there would not be enough sleeves or space in the garage roof, and either the bottles would fall from the garage beams or the number of stiff sleeves would give the game away.

Therapeutically, we would try to provide them with support and insight into their addiction and offer means by which they could swop their dysfunctional lifestyles for a more productive alternative.

Cora and Scott appeared to be doing well and impressed the group with advice and tips on how to beat the drink. I would call on the group members in their homes when I could, in between individual and group therapy. One day, I knocked on the door of Cora and Scott's house, and an unfamiliar woof sounded from within. I was welcomed with tea, and Bruce was introduced to me. He was quite a sizable dog with a brown coat. He appeared to be a mature dog, not just in years but also in his nature. He sat obediently while Cora and Scott told me how they had come by him. He was obviously aware that we were all in admiration of him. Their family was complete.

The next time I visited, they were excited to get Bruce to fetch his suit. Bruce, albeit somewhat reluctantly, a bit like a child whose parents wanted to show him off, fetched the suit. It was tartan and consisted of a tartan coat and a matching tam o' shanter hat. Being Scottish, they were very pleased it was tartan and told me how they had bought it from a charity shop. Bruce was regaled in his suit and went along with the needs of his owners. They told me how proud they were of him. He was a popular talking point, and neighbours would pay attention to him and recognise him. Previously, the couple would avoid contact with their neighbours and try to maintain a very low profile. Because of their drinking, they wanted anonymity, but now, they enjoyed a new-found sense of belonging to the neighbourhood through Bruce. The daily exercise from walking was also beneficial to all three. So, all appeared to be going well. Bruce was more than a pet; he was the child they'd never had. But also, in a funny way, he had become their mature guardian and facilitator.

The next time I called, the curtains were drawn, and the house looked deserted. I knocked at the door, and Bruce barked, but there was no sign of Cora or Scott, though I sensed they were there. I peered through the letterbox and Bruce put his nose up to the opening – he remembered me. I shouted through the letterbox, "Cora, Scott! Open this door. I'm not going until you let me in!" After quite a while, a curtain moved, and then Cora came to open the door in her nightie, crying and very apologetic, followed by a very remorseful Scott. The house, instead of being neat and tidy, told the story – drink and empty bottles were lying around. I poured the remaining drink (whisky) down the toilet. Bruce was clearly very worried and kept looking at them and then turning to me. He seemed comforted that someone understood. I read them the riot act and asked how they could let themselves down so badly, let alone Bruce. Did not they feel any responsibility? Very shameful, they apologised, saying they had let everyone down – themselves, me and Bruce. We parted with appointments for them to see me the next day.

I was hopeful that this was a slip from which they could learn and then continue their life with Bruce and, hopefully, a better future. Maybe they would exploit work opportunities or even undergo retraining. But it wasn't to be. A short time later, Cora was back to her old ways. She contrived to be found stealing drink, ensuring she was caught on CCTV camera, and this was followed by a court case and the inevitable prison. Clearly, our treatment and intervention hadn't been sufficient or successful.

Ferrets

As a child, I had seen ferrets used by my family to flush out rabbits. Any meat, including rabbit meat, was a popular source of protein to eat during the Second World War when food, particularly protein, was limited. Rabbits were considered pests because they destroyed crops, so country families, such as my own, often kept ferrets to serve as both a means of obtaining food and to cope with pests. I was not a particular fan of these little stoat-like creatures – I didn't like the way they would bite and then try to draw blood.

I had made an appointment to see a family with a particular problem associated with a young boy one afternoon. I can't remember details about the boy, only perhaps feel some sympathy with the scant attention he perhaps received from a mother, who might just put her interest in the ferrets before her son. I knocked on the door and waited outside. These waits on the doorstep were in themselves ominous signs, indicating maybe disdain, fear or disrespect. Inevitably, one had a sense of reluctance, indicating a lack of collaboration when, despite an appointment, the waiting on the doorstep was very prolonged. On this occasion, after the initial knock and some considerable time later, a woman answered the door. She opened it very slightly and commanded, "Come in quickly! I'm feeding the ferrets." I followed her into the kitchen with some caution. She ordered me to take a seat in the middle of the kitchen on a stool, telling me not to move and to sit very still, or I would put the ferrets off their meal. I sat reluctantly motionless while the ferrets went around the worktops vying for liver, which was placed in various piles round the kitchen and which the ferrets ate voraciously. My presence had obviously not put them off their meal!

True to my predictions, it was very difficult to become involved with the mother of this child. She sabotaged all efforts for me to help her child. The alternative was to work with the boy, his GP and his school, when clearly the focus should have been on the dynamics operating within the home. The ferrets were a clear indication of the source of the difficulties and priorities within the home.

Snakes

In the building where the family therapy department was housed, there were also district nurses who would visit families with newly born babies. One day, one nurse came into the department, very concerned. She had visited a couple with a new-born baby to find a snake curled up in the baby's cot. She had asked the couple about this, and they told her it was their hobby to collect snakes. It was a tiger snake. They showed no concern. Asking if the snake might be venomous, the couple said, "No, the snake is only a baby." The district nurse returned to the health centre and made an urgent call to the centre in the UK concerned with poisonous reptiles. The reply was that the tiger snake is a very dangerous species from Australia and is most prevalent in areas of high population density. Before biting, they will act out a display where they flatten their necks and hiss. A bite from even a so-called baby could kill.

So much for just a harmless baby tiger snake! This was a similar situation to the ferrets, in that parents were fitting their children into their own interests, in this case, their pets. I am sure this behaviour is not related purely to pets; one can see families where hobbies are continued without compromise or adaption to maintain the welfare of the family.

Naturally, there is a flipside to this: the families as a whole can benefit from the possession of certain shared attributes in the form of interests, hobbies and caring for pets. However, as a therapist, I am aware that these can serve as valuable indications of serious distortions which are detrimental to the functioning of the family as a whole or to a child or individual member.

Siamese cats

I was again out and about, calling on various patients, on this occasion, an elderly alcoholic, Derek. He lived alone in a beautiful house overlooking the sea in Sussex. We were sitting in a lounge, he against a beautiful picture window with the sea sparkling beyond. We were deep in conversation about his life and his problem with drink. If I looked to my right, I had an uninterrupted view of the kitchen. While listening to Derek, my attention was drawn to movement in the kitchen. I did not want to appear disinterested in what Derek was disclosing, but since I knew he was alone in the house, I couldn't ignore an increasing amount of activity out of the corner of my eye! Not wanting to appear rude, I mentioned this to Derek. He said, "It's the cats. The one cat's feeding the other!" What they were doing was one cat would take the lead and keep jumping up trying to open the refrigerator door. He eventually disturbed the catch and the door sprang open. The second cat got into the fridge and they selected what they wanted, helping themselves from the contents. So, they were all happy. I presumed that when Derek was drunk, the cats, desperate for food, had learnt to fend for themselves.

A very large dog

I was asked to visit a family living in a remote area, concerning a girl about whom the school were worried. I found the address. The bungalow was surrounded by overgrown vegetation and weeds and looked dank and inhospitable. I knocked on the door. I was eventually invited into a very dark room by a rather sinister-looking woman. The focal point of the room was a fireplace where a grate was full of ashes with a single wisp of smoke curling up the chimney. The whole atmosphere was odd. I would not have been surprised to have been told it was the headquarters of a witch's coven. Even the girl's mother was unusual. She suited the room and the atmosphere: dark and drab with long, grey, unkempt hair.

The mother told me to sit down, pointing to one end of a sofa. It was one of those very old, worn-out sofas without springs which I have encountered before. As you try to sit, you wrongly predict and misjudge, by which time, it's too late – you hit the base inches from the floor with your knees level with your chin. In this precarious position, I tried to become composed as the therapist. The mother told me about the daughter, who had yet to return from school. The plan was to discuss her daughter's difficulty while we waited for her to walk from the school bus.

While concentrating on the mother and her story, I heard from another room a barking from what sounded like a big dog. Out of the corner of my eye, I saw a white cat jumping up to release the door catch and the mother mentioned in passing that the cat was letting the dog in. It is worth reinforcing here that this distraction could have been avoided by the mother if she were intent on cooperating with me and taking seriously the visit to help her daughter resolve her difficulties. But her attitude and behaviour were indicative and, therefore, important constituents of the assessment process I was undertaking.

Eventually, the cat did open the door, and the dog pushed from the other side and barged in. He was an enormous black dog. As a farmer's daughter, it takes a lot to faze me. But from my very lowly position on the couch with my knees up under my chin, I began to feel vulnerable. The dog reached up and put his huge paws on the side of the sofa and leaned over me menacingly. He towered above me, now growling and showing his teeth, his saliva dripping down beside me. I did become frightened; this dog was dangerous. The mother told me to 'sit tight'. I took her advice because I was too petrified to move. Then the mother said, "You're sitting on his jam sandwich!" I very slowly edged away from the dog and his sandwich. He pounced on the sandwich, and I made my getaway while he was eating it. I left as quickly as I could to the safety of my car, placing my jam- and saliva-covered coat on the back seat. I vowed never to visit again; they could see me at the clinic.

It was such an extraordinary experience, with the mother showing absolutely no concern, it almost felt as if I'd been set up.

Birds

Identical twins came to the drop-in centre for the under-25s. Sometimes, patients did not disclose initially why they had decided to attend, and the twins were an example. They appeared identical, with Cleopatra-style black hair cut in a stylish bob. They were both heavily made up with black eyeliner and mascara applied boldly and liberally and lashings of bright red lipstick. They were a striking couple. If I asked a question, they both waited for the other twin to do the talking. They would look at me and then look at each other, mistrustful that the other twin might disagree. To reach any meaningful dialogue was not easy. I sensed they were worried because they realised that they could not operate alone and that they needed another viewpoint to help them come to some sort of conclusion. They told me that they had both had boyfriends, but that it never worked.

They attended initial appointments in my office, but still without any clear understanding and articulation of their need to visit me. They were always punctual and very respectful and appeared to value our sessions, but I did not feel satisfied that I was getting to the cause of their concerns. Compared with other clients I was treating, the twins did not rate as urgent or serious, but I was also cautious because, sometimes, it takes time and trust for patients to disclose their problems. I decided to visit them in their flat to see if I could dig a little deeper and provide more help in their own surroundings. They had a downstairs flat in a large Victorian house on the fringe of the city. Having located their entrance, I knocked on the door and was welcomed warmly into their home. The room was very large with a particularly high ceiling. To my surprise, the room was full of parakeets cheeping happily, perching on furniture or flying around the room up on the ledges. They were everywhere. The noise was deafening. It was amazing. I could understand having a few, but there must have been a hundred or more. There was no way that it was possible to carry on a meaningful conversation. The next appointment was back at the clinic. Perhaps the twins just needed the peace and quiet of my consulting room?

Entering the homes of patients is a very privileged encounter and it does often provide an essential perspective in helping to understand the psychopathology. The very wide range of living conditions, styles and priorities provides a backdrop against which assumptions can be made. Some of these extreme examples suggest, or indeed even indicate, psychopathology. The extent to which the pets were indulged and cared for was often at odds with the patient's own lack of priority and personal health and welfare. For example, a heroin addict always bought her pet food before buying heroin for herself. Animals, for some, appear to 'complete the family' or divert their attention. Alternatively, to some patients, their pets placed them in a position of control which they could not exert elsewhere. Others would show preference to their pets before their own children.

There is a link between psychopathology and the variety, size, volume and numbers of pets. In some cases, the presence of pets appears dysfunctional and uneconomic, particularly when necessities for the family are neglected in favour of the acquisition and feeding of the pets. This was the case for one family who, despite many financial and dysfunctional difficulties, adopted a dog who needed costly surgery.

However, the stories of companionship and the benefits pets bring to so many outweighs the negativity. For example, Oscar the cat sensed death in a home for patients with dementia. Oscar is an example of pets having a self-selected role. He was a two-year-old kitten, who, the staff observed, would visit dying patients. He would stay with them curled up beside them on their bed until they died. Staff confirmed he was always right, alerting them, when sometimes they did not know death was imminent.

The relationship between pets and their owners and the part they play in therapy is popular. Dogs particularly bring comfort to children and to adult patients by visiting hospitals. Stroking and watching them behave in an uncontrived, natural manner appear to bring comfort to the ill. No doubt, they form a bridge between the irrationality of abnormality and normality in its most natural and unpretentious form.

However, what I am suggesting is that the relationship between psychopathology and an unusual choice of pet is indicative. The behaviour of the client towards the pet, and sometimes the behaviour of the pet towards the environment in which it has had to adapt, can be illuminating. While the adults with psychopathology can make choices, the children of these adults cannot. Observing children fitting into circumstances beyond their control with parents acting in clearly irresponsible ways towards them was of great concern. As I have intimated, the expectation of me as a therapist was to treat those referred and to communicate to the referral source my findings (e.g. Simon is suffering from an emotional disorder. The school complains that he is a destructive influence in the classroom, is hyperactive and unable to concentrate, etc.).

It never sat comfortably with me to name Simon and others like him as the patient, when 99% percent of the time these children were just reacting to the dynamics operating within the family. The parents were so often parents with personality disorders and the children had to fit into two conflicting worlds, an eccentric home environment and school, with its semblance of normality. For some, this was an unsustainable position.

Chapter 14
At the Sharp End

An unexpected phone call triggered a chain of events which, for me as a family therapist, led to work challenges on a monumental scale. The outcome was a new model of working with patients who had referred themselves. If they had been referred along the normal channels, they would have been diagnosed as personality disorders. The service which resulted was a 'bottom-up service' that was driven by the patients and their identified needs.

On reflection, the successful intervention called into question the whole diagnostic criteria of 'personality disorder' and the implication that it is untreatable, a belief held by some. The patients were resilient, motivated and innovative – pure gold for a therapist.

Having first served as a therapist and then a manager, I was led by this experience to propose a paradigm shift that was possible and achievable by the example described below: a move away from the expectations engendered by the NHS in the UK, whereby health is dependent on the welfare system, to one where health is the responsibility of the individual. I do not feel that welfare necessarily equates with health and that the NHS can undermine personal responsibility. Attitudes towards maintaining health and the resilience to achieve health should be central goals perpetuated from childhood through to maturity. The service described demonstrates that from its inception through to successful discharge, the patient's personal characteristics are available to tap and employ to bring about change in the most challenging cases.

I received a call from a medical consultant who explained that she wanted funding for her research on unintended pregnancies. One of the requirements on the application form was a named person who would take care of matters of a social or psychological nature which might require help. She was making light of her request by saying, "There's probably nothing likely to occur. I just need your name." The second requirement was that she needed statistical help with the research. At the time, I was working full-time as a family therapist with a large caseload. I was also a wife and mother. I felt I needed her to understand that any undertaking on my part had to be weighed up with my capacity to cope with any additional workload.

My first task was to disavow her belief that my involvement would be in name only and to explain that in my experience, an unintended pregnancy could be symptomatic of a variety of difficulties. I needed to explain to her further that in family therapy, the object is not just to focus on the individual referred but to view and assess the problem within the familial context, even seeing the whole family as sick. In other words, the interactions within the whole family become the focus, and the aim is to try to get to the very root of the problem. The unintended pregnancy may be just a part and symptomatic of wider psychopathology and social implications. For example, a referral was received to attend a crisis situation in a local high school. A girl had become hysterical following the showing of a film of an abortion procedure. The girl, Holly, had just had an abortion. She had known that her mother and stepfather wanted another child and she became pregnant to provide them with the child, only for her stepfather to take her for an abortion.

The statistical analysis, the second part of the deal, would be much easier to manage.

I eventually agreed to what was a voluntary arrangement and said that I would help with both her requirements as best I could. I could never have realised just what would happen and the consequences! Not long after the consultant had obtained her funding and she was busy beginning her research, I got a phone call. It wasn't via the usual channels, but it came from a telephone box. Furthermore, it wasn't associated with an unintended pregnancy. The caller was a young man in trouble, who wanted help to withdraw from drugs. He had to keep putting money into the telephone, so our conversation was disjointed. Sensing that the caller was frightened and perhaps too terrified to use a telephone in the usual manner, I quickly suggested we meet in a church, somewhere private, safe and a centralised, local landmark. I suggested a time when I was free, and he readily agreed.

This was the first of many clandestine meetings with patients who, in preference to the established provision, wanted to choose who they wanted to help them and where. I learnt a valuable lesson that there is a need for treatment/help – call it what you will – to be tailored to the needs of the individual. It needs to be flexible, and sometimes, just providing blanket approaches and services does nothing to reach and meet the needs of some patients. Not responding and meeting their needs means a lost opportunity to turn lives around.

The first patient

I found the young man waiting nervously, sitting in a pew in a darkened part of the church. I never knew how he got my telephone number, but I presumed it was associated with a flyer which was offering confidential help to pregnant girls.

His story was as follows: He was 20, slightly built with dark, unkempt, greasy hair, pale, unshaven and timid. He had left school and gone to university where he found the change from home to university difficult. He was offered cannabis and immediately felt uplifted. He progressed and belonged to a drug-taking peer group. He then recognised he was in a dangerous, downward spiral and that his habit was becoming unsustainable. His studies deteriorated until he was finally asked to leave.

He returned home from university, ashamed. He then lived with his elderly parents but could not afford the cannabis to which he was addicted. After several clandestine meetings with him, I eventually asked if I could visit his parents, and surprisingly, he agreed. They were a sad old couple, quite ancient and very worried about their only son. They had no idea of their son's predicament. Previously, they had been proud of him as he was doing well academically, and they felt that he was assured of a future that they had never had. However, he had started threatening them for money, which clearly, they couldn't afford (I got the impression that if they had the money, they would have given it to him). The patient's parents needed protection. I remember the old mother taking me to her son's bedroom, pleased to show me that her son was taking an interest in biology. But what she showed me was cannabis growing profusely!

The outcome was good. He eventually resumed university and did well.

I continued to get referrals – so many that I couldn't manage them all. Clearly, the anonymity of the clandestine meetings and the confidentiality indicated an important and compelling alternative to the established NHS and Social Services, provided via doctors, clinics and voluntary bodies. Although most of the patients I saw at that time were wanting to get off addictions (i.e. drugs, drink, gaming, etc.), there were also many other problems which covered the whole spectrum of the so-called personality disorders and deviant behaviour, such as bestiality, together with some neurotic obsessions, phobias, etc.

There appeared to be an information web working beneath the norms of society, reaching those who wanted to abstain and to get them the help they needed – but on their terms. I found this intriguing because each patient was very wary and untrusting. It seemed unlikely that they were informing each other. I could only assume they were searching, and their antennae were acutely active and picking up the part of the flyer (for unintended pregnancy) which assured anonymity.

This was a different way of working for me, I was learning. I never knew how the patients had found me, but they did. They knew, recognised and appreciated that they were deviant. However, they appeared to want to have the sort of help which gave them control without becoming patients in the normal manner. One factor I learnt was that the assessment process was a two-way affair. I needed to assess them, but the stakes were so high for them that they needed to assess me. They were assessing my ability to help them, my strength to withstand their problems, my wisdom and expertise to bring about change, but also trying to determine if they could trust me. Testing me out was a feature in each initial meeting. I've mentioned this in a previous case study, but it's worth repeating here: One patient started the initial conversation by saying, "I've fractured a man's skull. I've broken arms!" as if to intimidate me, but also implying the question, 'Can you cope with me?' The age range was wide: the youngest self-referral was eight, the oldest, a senior citizen. It was risky for me and for them; some were in trouble with the law for drug pushing, debt repayment, etc.

What happened next?

Need and demand dictated that things could not go on as they were; it was unsustainable. The meetings were in churches, car parks, doss houses (usually hotels that were no longer viable), cafes – anywhere. That first meeting was so crucial for gaining a chance to help them turn their lives around. I can't emphasise how important that first meeting was. I knew that if I did not add up in their assessment of me, there would be no second chance to help them – no second meeting.

A base with facilities was indicated where someone could man the telephone. Consequently, in short, a new service was born, driven by and centred on the needs of these particular patients. At the time, the government was very worried about HIV and Aids, so any initiative making a provision for the treatment and prevention of drug addiction with its link to the use of needles was encouraged and alarmist money was made available. A case was made, and funding became available. A house was purchased and a base was established. I continued to see patients, initially, wherever it was safest, but then gradually, as a trust was built up between us, they would venture to the house/clinic, and I would see them in my room.

How did it work?

This was a new way of working with psychopathology: the patients made the running. They weren't referred with the usual case notes, history, symptoms, suggested diagnosis and medication. Furthermore, there were no resources: no beds for cold turkey, no prescription pad, no social workers, no back-up team. It was, to put it mildly, clandestine. We, the patient and I, had nothing but our combine resources. Fear was omnipresent at every new encounter. It was risky for us both: for them, in case they were recognised, and particularly so for the drug users. If the pushers found out, they would take their revenge by shooting them in the kneecap, which was the current reprisal for breaking rank. Sometimes, they continued buying drugs just to keep the drug pushers at bay. For me, it was also risky. I was venturing into underworlds I had never encountered before. Nobody knew where I was or what I was doing – I had no supervision.

On one occasion, a drug user wanted to prevent drugs being shipped and asked me if I would notify the police confidentially.

I agreed and made the call. I was subsequently contacted by the drug squad leader. The conversation started amicably enough with me passing on the date and location of the shipment to the local harbour. He then asked to speak to me again and asked where I had got the information. I told him I couldn't divulge the source. Things then turned nasty, and he threatened to subpoena me! Quite naturally, this was uncomfortable since confidentiality was at the root of the success. So, I just said that he could try but I'd never divulge the source. He didn't try again.

Developing a method fit for purpose

It became incumbent upon me to develop a method which very broadly involved three defining modalities: the past, the present and the future. I'd listen to the patient's immediate situation during the first meeting and then I would explain to them how I worked and what was required of them. They were then sent to think of the commitment they needed to make. So, this was a real departure from the usual expectation of patients. Patients usually can expect the entire service to kick in, and to provide all the support and resources they need in every aspect of their lives.

Initially, these patients needed to make a decision of their readiness to make a commitment to work towards established goals. Success of reaching the goal was based on the combined commitment of the patient and myself; our only resource was our united effort. I felt it very important to start this way, nurturing them and exploring what my expectation of them could be. How far could I go? The contract went like this: 'If you want help with your problem, I will give you a hundred percent, but I'll expect a hundred percent from you. The journey will be a journey of discovery the hardest and the most difficult but also the most exciting and rewarding journey you'll ever take!' I further explained that they would, at times, rebel, become defensive and test me out. That I accepted, but I would make sanctions such as cancelling an appointment. They could always resume, but because I had to be efficient to be effective, I was strict. If they agreed to this contract, we would start together, aiming to start a journey, weathering the ups and downs until finally, the patient could manage alone and could be discharged – not just limping along on the fringes of society, but ready to use the huge power they had generated by overcoming the initial problem to benefit themselves and society.

Malnourishment and adversity

On some occasions, the patients with addiction would be undernourished, so I would recognise that they needed to understand what powered the body apart from drugs and alcohol. I would explain that they needed to become healthy by living and respecting their bodies. This harks of mothering, which it was – some of them had never been mothered!

I used the same so-called 'model' whatever the situation because it worked! Why did it work? It worked, I feel sure, because I was looking to mobilise the very same latent power which had caused them to self-treat, turn to drugs and to depart into deviance in the first place. These patients were different: independent and resourceful. My conviction was that so often they turned to mind-altering substances or so-called deviant behaviour in an effort to feel better. A child who is trying to cope against a background of marital instability and is suddenly offered magic mushrooms feels immediately transformed. Most of the patients were victims of this effort to self-treat. Very importantly, they still had belief in themselves, and it was my job to reinforce that belief and desire.

Personality disorder?

Against this background, I've often felt uncomfortable with the diagnosis of personality disorder because there is a belief by some that patients so labelled cannot be treated. While nearly all the patients who referred themselves to this service could be diagnosed as having a personality disorder, I found them motivated, responsive, innovative and very exciting to work with. I am reminded of Jung's gold to be found amongst the trash of the unconscious. Yes, they probably were untreatable if their own resources weren't mobilised and they weren't given a chance of an olive branch! But if they were, they were gold for any therapist.

Psychotherapy and the importance of narrative

Initially, an important ingredient of this joint approach was, undoubtedly, the confidentiality that was the trigger for the clients' gamble to disclose to me the nature of their difficulties. So, confidentiality had to be observed. In practice, this meant never taking notes and never going behind their backs. Another necessary ingredient was the respect we, as therapists, owe to our patients (i.e. never taking a telephone call during 'their' time, never keeping them waiting, reinforcing the value of our respect for them).

Another ingredient was to hear their story, to listen to their narrative. Perhaps it was the first time anyone had listened to them. This was sacred and intense. I was looking for milestones to help me understand what had brought them to the point where they were desperate enough to see me. For them, it was to make sense of their life so far. This dialogue would begin not with 'Why are you drinking, drug taking, etc.? How many pints? How much?' But instead, asked questions like, "What are your earliest memories? Right then, what happened next?" The conversation would proceed by probing into the past, delving, reaching agreeable conclusions, explaining hurts that had derived, perhaps, from a mother's or father's point of view.

The need to recognise deficits

Generally, I was dealing with developmental deficits, in that these patients had experienced skewed upbringings. As was shown in the case study on William, patients belonged to peer groups where the pressure and need to belong meant they needed to become involved in deviance, theft and anti-social behaviour. Therapy had to deal not only with the recognition that leaving the peer group would create a vacuum which had to be filled, but also that because they possessed educational and social deficits, they had to be fit and prepared to enter another social group with needs to conform within society. So, each session would hop back and forth from the past to the present and the future.

Another final factor was that they had to do homework. There were sanctions if they didn't attend the next appointment having done their homework to my satisfaction. The homework gave them a bridge linking each session. Homework started simply but would, gradually, become more demanding and more involved as they progressed. It began with a simple task, such as 'keep a note of what you have eaten (paper and pencil provided), and we'll discuss it next time'. Finally, homework would involve something like agreeing to contact the college and arrange to see the head of this or that course or to go for a job interview. I always started a session by asking them if they had done their homework.

When I realised what was necessary for the patients to integrate into the society from which they had been marginalised, I started a group. The purpose of the group was to take them out and do something enjoyable but also to learn to behave respectfully while in the company of others. It sounds unimportant, but just something simple like gathering up the cups after coffee and getting the appreciation of the café owner was demonstrating that society responds to acts of thoughtfulness, something they would have spurned in their previous peer group of nonconformists where deviance was the ticket to belong. However, I was aware that bringing together my patients in a group had its real dangers, and I risked them forming a splinter group. But it never happened.

Considering the future and preparing them for the next leap was exciting on the one hand, but daunting on the other. They often had had no schooling to speak of, so the future had to be confronted on all sides. There were issues related to every-day living and every conceivable hurdle had to be confronted. Earning a living and a future career were the ultimate aims, tempered naturally by the aptitudes, abilities and resilience of each individual. Evening classes and night school were options but so was applying for jobs. Being interviewed and making suggestions about appropriate clothing and appearance had to be discussed. Sometimes, giving them dummy interviews was appropriate.

But this is where the particular gold of the patients shone through. Given that their appearance began to improve, they felt better, they were living healthily and they were innovative. They did not expect care, so they would embrace the challenges with solutions. Their past had made them streetwise and resilient. These skills they mobilised and used to best effect to further their futures.

Inevitably, the day would come when I knew I should broach the subject of discharge. This was difficult for me and for them, but it was akin to the fledgling that needs to make their first flight and move away from the nest; it was a necessary event. It was the culmination of the contract between us and returned to them the power and expectation that if they could come this far on this very difficult journey, they could reach for the sky – and some of them did. I was very moved when they returned to tell me how far they had gone. As mentioned above, one patient tracked me down and placed £250 on the table saying, "That's for you to help someone like me."

On a more reflective note, I was asked to meet on a monthly basis with other therapists who were employed to cope with dependency at a regional level. It took a day out of my month, and I didn't know how justifiable it would be. Time was always at a premium.

We, who were intended to provide therapy and to prevent the proliferation of drugs and HIV, were asked by the experts in the county responsible for monitoring services to give them the numbers of referrals each month. They needed to justify funds by collecting statistics (i.e. numbers of treatments). 'We', the so-called therapists, would sit in a circle of approximately eighteen people and each would report on the number of new patients and the number of treatments given. The striking factor for me was that I was the only member of the group who could report new patients on a regular basis. The other therapists had to use their time on prevention. Managers will always want money to fund such initiatives, but I hope I can convince that this isn't the main need. What's at the heart of this initiative is tapping the motivation of the individual, both the patient's and the therapist's.

The next chapter is a brief retrospective reflection following experience as a therapist, manager and then medical researcher in the NHS in the UK. Examples are used which demonstrate how the integrity and purpose of a managerial system can be undermined. As it is for health – to be forewarned is to be forearmed, and prevention is the best policy.

Chapter 15
Managemental Malady

"Stop! Cut it there!" shouted the principal. The lights in the auditorium suddenly went on, illuminating the previously darkened proceedings, and everyone altered their mode to what's happening? What's wrong?

"You can't ask that," the principal continued. He was looking at me incredulously. My crime was that in my assigned role as an interviewer on a recruitment panel, I had dared to ask the applicant, among other questions, how many days she'd had off sick in the previous year.

To explain the situation, I had won a place at a university on a post-graduate rehabilitation course to study two focal topics: research and management systems. This initiative was to prepare senior professionals in the field to become managers following the Griffiths report. This report was commissioned to address the urgent necessity to stop the bottomless purse of funding and make the NHS in the UK efficient and effective by adopting a managerial system. The research component was charged with weeding out the subjectivity of treatments, replacing treatments which did not pass scientific scrutiny with those which were demonstrably shown to be effective. In others words, they were seeking objectivity.

The management component was to herald, facilitate and instigate budgetary accountability, replacing the old system. The belief was that money would be saved and that the health service could continue as a healthier and, more importantly, sustainable system. It is worth noting that the NHS is on a par with a national treasure – any political party which in any way sabotages the NHS is politically doomed.

I was more interested in the research component than the managerial systems, but I could see the need for the realism and that the two-pronged approach was both complementary and necessary. My background was as a farmer's daughter, so the practicality of business decisions and a certain realism were part of my DNA. In my own realm as a therapist, up to that point, there had been no link between treatment and the proven outcome. As an example, massage was part of the treatment, but apart from the patients enjoying it, nobody could verify that it was effective. Objectifying various treatments using research techniques was therefore necessary.

The course was designed to teach management skills to those who were the most likely candidates to hold the first managerial posts in the new management system. So, here I was on this new course aimed at propelling therapists into a new age, backed up with realistic costing, hiring and firing personnel – a management system. They were adopting the very system used in industry, concerned with cutting out superfluous and non-essential expenditure, where profit margins could produce profit. Very basically, the ethos of the managerial system was sensible and resembled that of a farm, and the farm which had been part of my background could not afford 'hangers on' and had to cut out the sentimentality. For example, a cow which was barren could not contribute and had to be culled. Everything on the farm had to be justified, including my own position. I had from an early age needed to contribute. As my age and my height changed, my responsibilities grew commensurably. I had to milk a cow both before school and when I returned from school. I was not to do homework, but to do what was considered 'real' work. School was a statutory edict, tolerated but not encouraged.

So, against this background and moving forward in my life and needing to progress, here I was with other mature professionals taking advantage of their own futures, the needs of the country and the treatment of their patients. They were a very likeable group, and we all enjoyed being back learning and embracing the university life again. We had all worked in clinics, hospitals and departments with a responsibility for the rehabilitation of the patients. So, to be in one another's company learning and comparing notes and experiences was exhilarating.

That morning in the lecture theatre, a small part of the assessment for the management section of the course was concerned with recruitment procedure. It was called 'Hiring and Firing' and entailed the following:

- the formulation of a job description;
- compiling the advertisement for the job;
- arranging the interviewees;
- the interview;
- the letter providing the result to the applicants.

On this particular day, we were being filmed and assessed as we carried out the interviews. We had done our background work, pored over the applications in search of the ideal client necessary for the position to be filled and with the skills needed. We had written succinct advertisements in journals and periodicals. We then decided on the interviewers. Next, we decided the shortlist. Lastly, we had booked the venue. My assignment in all this was, as I have mentioned, to question each applicant on their present welfare, circumstances, hobbies, etc., in a kind and diplomatic manner. My colleagues on the panel kicked off with their areas of inquiry, and then it was my turn. The dramatic beginning, when the filming was stopped and the lights suddenly went on, was a shock not just for me but for everyone else. I was not credited with being dogmatic or assertive, just the reverse. Nevertheless, with hindsight, it was indicative. I was also shocked but not dramatically so; I was more interested.

Why? And what was the reason my question, which was merely about absenteeism, had caused so dramatic a reaction? Wasn't this at the heart of the need to save? Wasn't absenteeism rife in the NHS? Didn't everyone know that staff would ring in sick on Fridays or Mondays to prolong the weekend? Didn't we all know the various strategies employed to get out of our responsibilities? Didn't we all know of staff supposed to be driving to see patients in the community and not keeping their appointments so that they could do their shopping on the way? Hadn't we heard of midwives who would turn up to a mother and her new-born baby at 11 am just ready for a smoke and a coffee that the poor mother would provide after she had bathed and attended to the baby?

If I were a manager who had undertaken to provide a service within a budget, wouldn't I need to know everything about my staff before I employed them to ensure I could provide an effective, efficient service within budget? I dug in my heels, realising that the lecturers had no experience in running a business at all. I argued there and then that if someone was continually off sick, the burden of their absence would be carried by other staff! Furthermore, if I had to recruit agency staff, I would soon be in budget deficit. However, there was no agreement, and I was treated as if I were a criminal. The filming was continued. That instruction 'stop there!' should have had greater impact; it should have alerted me that here was a system which was the antithesis of what I had been immersed in on the farm. Sadly, I did not heed the warning. I was subsequently offered a management job, which I unwisely took, only to find similar situations arising.

Changing from one system to another (NHS versus managerial NHS) is predictably initially wasteful, inefficient and ineffective. In the old system, the matron was responsible for running the hospital while the doctors were accountable for the patients. I, along with occupational therapists, physiotherapists, etc., was state-registered but supplementary to medicine (paramedics), meaning, the patients were the responsibility of the doctors who devolved treatment to the paramedics. However, in the managerial system, the doctors lost their control and the matrons were replaced by managers – many managers. In essence, the tight system was replaced by many more managers, mostly nurses and paramedics, who knew nothing about management with its jargon and inherent procedures and implications, not to mention the necessary business savvy. This dilution from a matron who ran her hospital with dedication and military precision on the one hand, and the doctors who could dictate what they wanted and needed to treat, was replaced by an inferior system that was doomed to fail.

The altercation I caused was at the heart of the problem

The caring professions at their core attract self-selected carers; the NHS is made up of an amalgam of such people. Sickness is their business, their attraction, their life. I was asked as a favour to help a nurse prepare for an interview, and she was preoccupied with illness: in herself, in her family, even her pets. She made it her business to nurse everyone and everything. She advised radical management to everyone, urging them to make appointments to visit the doctor, even for trivial complaints, or to get second opinions, when they weren't indicated, etc. She herself was always off sick, as were her family. Her profession was being a nurse; her life was being a nurse.

Her request to me was to help her get a promotion and to become a sister in an outpatient department. She had applied for promotion before but was never successful. She appealed to me, asking why she had been overlooked. She didn't understand. The dummy interview started off with me asking questions that I would need to ask if I were a manager making the selection.

When I broached her own health, she was in her element – here was a subject which captivated her. She listed her ailments and their treatment, clearly animated. She told me she had been off sick for four months in the previous year. How could I possibly ignore this information if I as the manager was responsible for providing the out-patient service? Even though I went to great lengths to sympathetically explain to her that her interview technique was flawed, she thankfully failed to get the job.

Discussion

This brief account demonstrates from personal experience in the 'caring profession' how in delivering a service, in this case healing and care, there is a recognised need to accept a management strategy and structure. However, it is also acknowledged and to be expected that if the integrity of the whole system is executed on skewed foundations, the purpose and outcome are compromised. It, therefore, follows that it is indeed imperative and healthy to speculate on how and in what circumstances compromise may occur. Self-selection in all walks of life is generally accepted as positive. However, self-selection within a profession may undermine the function and integrity of the system. This is particularly relevant in the so-called caring professions which either consciously or unconsciously import entrenched personal needs into the system. The lessons learnt are that management systems can undermine the very function they are intended to provide, and furthermore, seemingly highly focused personnel with the same characteristics can sabotage the system.

Years later, the unrealistic unsustainable NHS system is still in crisis. It is a safety net for every expectation, whether it is a medical, social or mental condition, providing an ever-open door that encourages reliance and discourages self-responsibility and resilience. While it embraces 'every need', it is unable to cater for the core need for which it was originally aimed – to heal the sick. It is a sick system.

As a researcher, therapist and manager wearing various hats, as it were, I found my work interesting but at the same time confusing. I really didn't belong anywhere specifically. I could never put my feet comfortably under a desk and enjoy a certain complacency. The patients, on the other hand, were intriguing. They were the same, possessing bodies minds, but were unique individuals. Listening to their stories triggered the hypotheses I subsequently formulated.

As a psychotherapist and therapist, my first task was to get the trust of my patients, and the second was to get on their wavelength, to gain insight into their past and their present crisis which had brought them to me. Only then could I plan with them how we would work together. My article titled *The Sharp End* (2018) gives a more explicit idea of how this worked.

Chapter 16
Resilience, Confrontation and Advice

Resilience is that ineffable quality that allows some people to be knocked down by life and come back stronger than ever, rather than letting failure overcome them. It's what Rutter (1999) called steeling.

When I am connecting, engaging with my patients particularly for the first time, there are a number of both conscious and unconscious processes at work. Early on, I'm listening for a narrative which shows resilience, indicating how robust the patient is and when is it safe to confront and get the show on the road, as it were. There is so much evidence that lies behind the greatest minds and their feats. Adversity is what powered the engine to reach unsurpassed achievement. As a therapist, I'm interested in whether my patients have any of these attributes which I can use to empower them, not just in the short-term but to benefit themselves and society in the long-term. If I can locate these sparks and ignite a flame, then the journey between us is going to be one of excitement for us both.

My sessions with my patients could also be confrontational. The patients have to be confronted with issues which could potential jeopardise their progress and future. Usually, they recognise their wrong choices, but on occasions, for their own good and progress, I would need to confront. Therapists who dodge confrontation, in my opinion, should not be therapists; they do not possess the necessary resilience themselves. Similarly, for my patient's sake, I would need to advise on a certain course of action. I could always cope with these various issues, such as confrontation and advise in a considered, sensitive manner. I could foresee them arising, so I would be prepared; but nevertheless, the need was always for the welfare of the patient, which entailed me to be in control. Therapists and health professionals are rightly wary of litigation, and they will be heavily influenced by this threat. Society has, in some ways, gone overboard with protection, rendering the real skills and tools to prevent and heal impotent. The tools remain in the toolbox, unused.

An example of where this was not the case was found in an organisation giving marriage guidance which asked me to consider being a counsellor. I was intrigued and went to discuss what they did and how they worked. But when discussing how they practised, I was told it was their policy to never discharge.

What this amounted to was that the patient/client made the running. If, for example, I couldn't confront, discharge or orchestrate the sessions, I would be in a position where I was impotent to use tools such as confrontation, advice and education. A paedophile might use sessions to enjoy discussing his perversion, and I would have no means of preventing what would be a reinforcing, collusive relationship with him. This practice might be suitable for some, but certainly not for me.

The next chapter is included because it demonstrates how science can work with intervention/therapy. This chapter can be excluded by those who are disinterested in scientific results and hypotheses testing. But to those interested, I will state that research was a very important adjunct to my life as a therapist. Instead of having just a moment of insight, exciting as that was, I could test it and either reject it or accept it.

Chapter 17
A Scientific Study: Self-Defeating Quotient as a Trait and Its Relationship with Neuroticism

This chapter describes a study conducted by the author which examined the extent to which multiple indices of self-destructiveness reflect a single unitary trait of self-destructiveness and the extent to which levels of this underlying trait are related to neuroticism. The results of a Structural Equation Model (SEM) provided support for a single-factor model of the Self-Defeating Quotient (SDQ). The results suggested that the relationship between the SDQ and neuroticism is quite strong. The study indicated that combining information from multiple measures into a composite trait measure, and using SEM to take measurement error into consideration, may provide a more accurate estimate of the strength of this relationship.

Introduction
The definition of a trait used for the purposes of this study is a genetically determined or a distinguishing quality or characteristic. A trait is not to be confused with state, which is a temporary way of interacting and dealing with the self and others (Spielberger, 1972). Understanding traits using the various assessment instruments allows comparisons and various inferences to be made about people in an objective, non-biased manner. Among the theorists who developed instruments to investigate traits are Hans and Sybil Eysenck (1975), who developed the Eysenck Personality Questionnaire, and Raymond Cattell (1965), who authored the Sixteen Personality Factor (16-PF) measure. Most of the assessment devices that result from trait theory adopt a self-report type test and incorporate an element which prevents faking good or lies which may comprise the integrity of the results. The main traits include disorder-

related categories such as depression, psychosis, histrionic (neurotic), introversion, masculinity/femininity (gender role) and hypochondriasis.

These assessment devices have provided a platform for gathering large amounts of information which can then be reduced using statistical factoring techniques allowing comparisons regarding a person's personality, interaction and beliefs about the self and the world. While different theorists may use different terminology, there is some consistency regarding factors or personality traits. Eysenck and Eysenck (1975) demonstrated Extroversion, Introversion, Neuroticism and Psychoticism, while there is some agreement between these traits and those now known as the Big Five, which are Openness to Experience, Conscientiousness, Extroversion/Introversion, Agreeableness and Neuroticism. For all of these five traits, people will fall somewhere on a continuum, with most falling somewhere in the middle.

The study examined the SDQ as a trait. Earlier research by the author (Thomson, 1996) found higher levels of premature mortality among individuals who had been diagnosed with clinical depression. Subsequent work (Thomson, 2014) sought to identify processes that mediated the relationship between depression and mortality. Clinically depressed individuals and those with elevated levels of Neuroticism (a risk factor for depression), had higher scores on the SDQ. Initial studies suggest that self-destructiveness is a trait, in the sense of being a stable and pervasive feature of personality (Kelley et al., 2005). Further, individuals who are high on this trait are also more likely to exhibit behaviours that have the potential to compromise physical health and lead to premature death. High levels of self-destructiveness have been found to be associated with higher levels of coronary-prone behaviour and drug use (Kelley et al., 2005), as well as suicidal ideation (Hopes & Williams, 1999). Higher levels of self-destructiveness are also related to poorer health-care habits, such as longer delays in initiating screening tests for cancer (Kelley et al., 2005), and higher risk-taking behaviour (Kelly, Rollings, & Harmon, 2005).

The study by Thomson (2014) utilised discrepancy scores between real and ideal behaviours to assess levels of self-destructiveness. Higher levels of neuroticism were related significantly to discrepancy scores in the following domains: emotional well-being, community affairs, personal habits, developmental contexts and social control. Two questions that arise from the results of this earlier investigation are addressed below. First, to what extent do the relationships between levels of self-destructiveness in the specific domains noted above reflect an underlying relationship between a general trait of self-destructiveness and neuroticism?

In order to fully address the previous question, a methodological issue in the use of discrepancy scores to measure traits was considered. Discrepancy scores may systematically underestimate the true strength of the relationship between variables. Cronbach (1990) discrepancy scores are vulnerable to the effects of measurement error. When the difference between two correlated scale scores is computed, the resulting discrepancy between scores retains the same amount of random measurement error that the original scale scores had, but less true score variance (since true score variance in one measure has been subtracted from true score variance in the other). To the extent that discrepancy scores include random measurement error, computation of the correlation between a discrepancy score and another variable will be attenuated (i.e. the computed correlation will be lower than the correlation between true scores) (Nunally & Bernstein, 1994).

To address the issue of self-destructiveness as a trait, while considering the role of measurement error, the study utilised SEM (Joreskog, 1993) to examine the relationship between measures of self-destructiveness and neuroticism. To better understand the extent to which measures of self-destructiveness reflect a unitary trait, SEM was employed. SEM also provided an opportunity to examine the relationship of self-destructiveness to psychological adjustment after taking into consideration the effects of random measurement error in fallible indicators (Joreskog, 1993).

Method
Sample

The study utilised data from 159 participants. A substantial portion of the sample received psychiatric care for depression: 34.2% of the sample received treatment for depression, while the remaining 65.8% of the sample served as normal controls. Females comprised 64% of the sample, while 36% were male. The median age of the study participants was 39 years old. With respect to employment status, 40.9% of the sample were employed full-time, 30.8% were employed part-time and 1.9% were self-employed. A further 6.3% were full-time students without employment, 10.1% were unemployed, 5.0% were disabled, 2.5% were retired and 2.5% were homemakers. Pre-existing medical conditions were present in 35.1% of the sample.

Procedures

The test group consisted of patients referred to a psychiatrist and diagnosed as depressed in an outpatient department. The questionnaires were enclosed in a stamped, addressed envelope and accompanied by an information sheet that explained the purposes of the study. Potential participants were informed that their involvement in the study was voluntary, that they could withdraw from the study at any time after they started and that responses to the survey would be anonymous. Every patient who was referred as possibly depressed by their GP was invited to complete a questionnaire while they awaited the consultation with the psychiatrist. Control subjects were not being treated for mental illness.

Instruments

Eysenck Personality Questionnaire

The Eysenck Personality Questionnaire (EPQ; Eysenck & Eysenck, 1975) consists of 90 yes-no items that are designed to measure three dimensions of personality: Neuroticism, Extroversion and Psychoticism. The measure also includes a Dissimulation Scale to screen out respondents who give distorted answers to appear socially desirable. The EPQ scales have shown high levels of reliability, both in terms of internal consistency and test-retest reliability coefficients (Eysenck & Eysenck, 1975). Alpha coefficients and test-retest correlations for the EPQ scales are higher than .8 across demographic sub-samples. The dimensional structure of the EPQ has proved to be robust in numerous factor-analytic studies. Illustratively, a simple structure factor rotation yields three dimensions that are comprised, respectively, by the Neuroticism, Extroversion and Psychoticism items (Barrett & Kline, 1980). Further, these three dimensions appear to underlie the factor structure of many other widely used personality inventories (Kline & Barrett, 1983). Considerable evidence for the external validity of the EPQ dimensions has been provided by numerous studies relating differential performance on experimental tasks, as well as behavioural patterns in real-world settings, to levels of Neuroticism, Extroversion and Psychoticism (Eysenck, 1967).

Self-Defeating Quotient

The SDQ was developed by the author (Thomson, 2014) to assess factors that mediate the relationship between depression and premature mortality among depressed patients. Items for the SDQ were piloted with patients who were undergoing treatment for depression and were revised in consultation with treating psychiatrists. The SDQ consists of 33 statements describing elements of the respondents' behaviour and feelings and is administered in two parallel forms: one describing the extent to which the statement describes the actual behaviour or feelings of the respondent (the Now form), and the other indicating the Ideal level of each item (the Ideal form). The response scale used was a 100 mm line, which represented a continuum of response. Illustratively, the Control item asks participants to indicate how much control they have over 'things that made them feel optimistic and content'. Participants responded to this item by indicating whether they had 'total control or no control'. Subjects were asked to mark their response to each item on the line. Responses were coded from zero to 100. At the one extreme, the preferential state or behaviour was represented by a score of zero, while a negative response was indicated by a score of 100.

The scoring of the SDQ was based on factor analysis of the item ratings, as described by Thomson (2014). Four factorially based scores were computed for the SDQ-Now, and four parallel scales were computed for the SDQ-Ideal. The Emotions, Habits and Community scale was computed as the average rating of items dealing with control, initiative, contentment, stress, problems, temper, jealousy, elections, neighbours, country, community, diet, weight and debt. The Social Control scale was computed as the average rating for items dealing with honesty, caring, aggression, conservation, exercise, vandalism and destruction. The Developmental Contexts scale was computed as the average of items related to early education, adult learning, colleagues, childhood, work, family, family time, law and altruism. Finally, the Drugs, Alcohol, Smoking and Frustration scale was computed as the average rating of these four constituent items. A discrepancy score for each of the SDQ scales was computed by subtracting the SDQ-Ideal rating from the SDQ-Now rating. Higher discrepancy scores indicated that the SDQ-Now rating reflects a more negative evaluation of present circumstances compared with the SDQ-Ideal rating.

Results

Preliminary analyses examined the mean response of subjects to the EPQ and SDQ scales. The main analyses of the study then examined a causal model relating SDQ Now-Ideal dimensions to differential levels of Psychoticism, Neuroticism and Extraversion.

Sample Descriptives

Eysenck Personality Questionnaire

Of the 159 subjects who participated in the study, 125 provided complete data on the EPQ. Mean scores for the sample on the EPQ scales are shown in Table 1. Compared with the EPQ norms (Eysenck & Eysenck, 1975), scores on the Neuroticism scale were notably higher, as would be expected in a sample that is comprised predominantly of individuals with clinical depression.

Table 1. Descriptive Statistics for EPQ Scales

Scale	Mean	S.D.
Neuroticism	14.2	5.1
Extraversion	11.1	4.8
Psychoticism	3.2	2.3
Dissimulation	7.2	3.2

Self-Destruction Questionnaire

The valid sample size with respect to the four Ideal and four Now factors varied from 123 to 147, depending upon the factor in question. Mean scores for the SDQ items in Now and Ideal forms are shown in Table 2. Scale scores on the SDQ-Now form were higher than scores on the SDQ-Ideal form, indicating that, on average, subjects described their actual behaviour and feelings as less than ideal.

Table 2. Descriptive Statistics for SDQ Now and Ideal Scales

SDQ Scale	Now Mean	SD	Ideal Mean	SD
Emotions, Habits, Commun.	39.5	15.6	15.0	9.7
Social Control	26.6	14.0	10.41	0.5
Developmental Contexts	30.3	14.0	14.0	11.5
Drugs, Alc., Smoking, Frus.	28.7	15.9	14.5	11.3

SDQ Now-Ideal Discrepancy and Neuroticism

In order to examine the structure of the relationship between SDQ Now-Ideal Discrepancy scores and Neuroticism, SEM was employed.

The SEM model conducted tested a one-dimensional model of the relationship between self-destructiveness and neuroticism. Here, higher SDQ discrepancy scores on the Emotions, Habits and Community scale, Social Control scale, Developmental Contexts scale and Drugs, Alcohol, Smoking and Frustration scales were treated as indicators of a single unitary dimension of Self-Destructiveness, which in turn were used to predict differential levels of Neuroticism. This one factor model of the relationship between self-destructiveness and neuroticism indicated statistical significance with respect to the path between SDQ Discrepancy scores and Neuroticism, Beta = .980, $p < .001$. Perfect model fit was indicated in this case as this model was just-identified.

In order to aid in the interpretation of this model, parameter estimates are presented below. Standardised regression coefficients relating the latent dimension of Self-Destructiveness to the four SDQ discrepancy scores are shown in Table 3. Only the initial scale included in the analysis was related significantly to the SDQ discrepancy dimension. The strength of the relationship between the latent dimension and each SDQ discrepancy score can be assessed by computing the square of the standardised regression weight. Discrepancy scores in the Emotions, Habits and Community scale exhibited the strongest relationship with the latent dimension [Beta = -.636]: slightly over 40% of the variance in the Emotions, Habits and Community discrepancy score is accounted for by the latent dimension. Discrepancy scores on the other three SDQ scales also exhibited reduced, though still strong and statistically significant, associations with the latent dimension. The latent dimension of self-destructiveness accounted for approximately 9% to 20% of the variance in discrepancy scores on the remaining three factors.

Table 3. Standardised Regression Coefficients Relating SDQ Discrepancy Scales with Self-Destructiveness Dimension

SDQ Now Scale	Coefficient
Emotions, Habits, Commun.	636***
Social Control	347
Developmental Contexts -.	444
Drugs, Alc., Smoking, Frus.	306

Note.
   *** $p < .001$

Discussion
   The results of the study provided support for the view that self-destructiveness is a unitary trait. Consistent with this view, a one-factor model provided adequate fit to subjects' scores on a measure of self-destructiveness that encompassed multiple life domains. Findings from the structural equation modelling analysis also suggested that self-destruction and neuroticism are more closely associated than they might appear to be in simple correlational analysis. In an earlier investigation, Thomson (2014) found that higher discrepancy scores on all four SDQ dimensions were associated with higher levels of Neuroticism. The size of the significant bivariate correlations between these SDQ measures and EPQ Neuroticism scores ranged from .284

to .608 [median = .430]. This pattern of findings suggested that, individually, the SDQ scales accounted for between approximately eight and 18 percent of the variance in Neuroticism scores.

The effects of the self-destructiveness dimension on neuroticism may have been larger in the investigation for two reasons. First, composite levels of self-destructiveness, summed across multiple life contexts, might be more strongly related to neuroticism than are the more limited and specific aspects of self-destructiveness that are measured by single SDQ scales. In other words, the effects of self-destructiveness may be clearer when it is considered as a pervasive trait, rather than as a situation-specific issue. A second reason why the relationship between self-destructiveness and neuroticism might have been stronger in the investigation arises from the use of an analytic approach, structural equation modelling, which takes into consideration the effects of random measurement error in the discrepancy scores. Using SEM, the regression between self-destructiveness and neuroticism reflects an estimate of the effects of variation in true scores on the self-destructiveness measure. By contrast, the simple correlation between self-destructiveness discrepancy scores and neuroticism does not adjust for the attenuating effects of random measurement error on the correlation. Further investigation of the effects of discrepancy score measures should utilise SEM to assess the impact of measurement error on correlations.

Review

Previous to producing 'Sabotaging the Self', my research had been on subjects such as psychosomatic topics and hypotheses concerning personality and traits. These all arose out of interacting and treating patients. Once I had studied research methodology and understood statistics, it became only partly satisfying to treat; combining research and hypotheses testing and treatment was the icing on the cake.

Over time, I began to see the importance of traits and I would look to identify traits in each patient. I had the great privilege of having had help from Hans and Sybil Eysenck and their work on personality traits. I used their Eysenck Personality Questionnaire (EPQ) in relation to my landmark papers on stress (1980, 1986).

So, from then on, I would listen to patients and think how high their score on introversion, extraversion might be, or wonder what their psychoticism or neuroticism score, etc., would be. The correlates of the traits would signify their underlying personalities, which would allow me some latitude in understanding their psychopathology. Confrontation would be necessary, but only when the patients were ready to accept confrontation, which was a delicate matter.

Somewhere along the line while working in this manner, I could see an element in all of the patients which would work against them personally and against my efforts to turn their lives around. This self-sabotaging element would show itself to greater or lesser degree in everyone. Apart from confronting this element in the patients and making them aware of it to enable them to stop sabotaging themselves, I needed to confirm and verify its existence. Once I had gained this insight, the challenge was to prove the hypothesis. This involved a plan, a hypothesis, the development of a questionnaire (SDQ), a cohort, statistics and writing and reasoning the results. Furthermore, it required commitment and time, all in short supply. So, it took some time to actually gather all these elements and requirements together and then produce the paper. But I had the zeal to start and finish what I thought was a very important and missing trait.

Hans Eysenck did say when he was presenting Psychoticism with Sybil, "This is a trait, but it won't be the last." Naming the trait was another serious matter. The name needed to encapsulate succinctly what was happening.

My hope is that just as the Big Five are now well accepted generally, the Self-Sabotaging trait will join them, resulting in the Big Six. The need is to make conscious the fact that it's there. It will help people identify where and how they habitually sabotage their own best interest. This does not just include patients but also children, managers and everyone motivated to improve and know themselves. Thus, it will, hopefully, play an explanatory part in preventing psychopathology by making lives more manageable and more orderly, giving individuals more control to understand themselves. But until this new trait becomes consciously accepted as an existing and causative factor, we flounder around looking for external causes and react without any idea of the psychopathology underlying our own behaviour.

This scientific paper confirmed the existence within us all to a greater or lesser extent to sabotage ourselves. The next chapter is concerned with sabotaging family events, changing them from being happy occasions of celebration to occasions for feuding, negative behaviour, which represents another style of sabotaging.

Chapter 18
Vulnerability

Have you ever noticed that when you're preoccupied and anxious about the day, you make a mistake, say, knocking over a mug of coffee, the coffee spills and you attempt to wipe it up which makes you late? You then forget to check your bag, which makes you even more late, and this starts a chain reaction of mishaps (like falling dominoes) and further vulnerability. However, vulnerability is the result of various causes.

I felt compelled to write on the state of being vulnerable, which is defined as being able to be easily hurt, influenced or attacked. My contributions have generally focused on medical research and the case studies of patients. The medical research quenched my appetite to search for truths and objectivity. The case studies allowed me to share my involvement with patients as a family therapist.

It's not an exaggeration to say that every patient is vulnerable to a greater or lesser extent when they are ill – and not just psychologically but physically also. As therapists, our job is primarily to restore order. We need to know what is physically or mentally wrong with our patients to engage with them, deliver the treatment and lead them towards recovery. They come to us for our help and expertise, and we often become relied upon, trusted and respected by our patients. With experience, we are able to 'get the picture' of a patient and his/her diagnosis, and navigate our way towards improvement and order. It becomes second nature when treating a defined diagnosis. But how often do we fall short and do not deliver the comprehensive care needed? How often do we fail to appreciate and fully understand the plight of the patients entrusted to our care and the full ramifications of their illness and the disorder within their lifestyles and circumstances by failing to consider items beyond the diagnoses and treatment which make a difference?

Furthermore, by failing to see the whole picture, we can hinder the recovery process.

In this chapter, I have set myself the task of discussing vulnerability, which amalgamates my interests, uniting both the objectivity of research and the generalised predicament of living today in the twenty-first century. There has seldom been a time when we have become more consciously aware of this generalised feeling of being vulnerable. Whether it is due to the potential impact of environmental catastrophes, such as meteorites bombarding our planet; global catastrophes, such as tsunamis, hurricanes and wildfires; being at the mercy of terrorists; or, perhaps due to more personal biopsychosocial catastrophes, such as illness, work-related or relationship difficulties, such as divorce; or the vulnerability of financial markets. Thus, to avoid and remedy the state of being vulnerable, it is imperative that it is understood by being aware and having the ability to predict and the wisdom to prevent it.

In days gone by, sages were respected and their wisdom and guidance were regarded, but today, we live in a more spontaneous, reactionary world in response to catastrophic occurrence. Time for contemplation and thinking things through is in short supply. Mobile phones are almost an additional part of the body; we are ready to communicate with the world but the phone replaces the wisdom of consideration and results in knee-jerk reactions. This reliance increases vulnerability as we begin to lose the ability to assess and to be able to consider what priorities and decisions are best for the individual.

So, what is it like to be personally vulnerable?

It ranges from being just unpleasant to being just unable to bear psychic pain. We can be easily hurt personally or collectively, depending on the situation and individual differences. We can be wrongly influenced and leave ourselves open to attack. It is personified, as we are left feeling alone, irrespective of the amount of support we might receive, and nevertheless, having to be on the frontline and live the fear and the consequences of making decisions. It's also about making decisions at the wrong time, too quickly and in the wrong circumstances or making the wrong decision because of hopelessness and loss. An example of this is a young woman who loved visiting her aunt, but when the aunt was brutally murdered, the young woman emigrated, abandoned the life she was building. Vulnerability is about having nothing and going into a relationship, hoping for a rainbow.

Another example is the vulnerable child who comes out of the school gates looking tired, pale and drawn and is immediately noticeable to the drug pusher who is trying to cultivate the vulnerable as potential buyers and who offers the child drugs. The child experiences a feeling of euphoria and he/she is hooked.

Fear of attack and reprisal leads to vulnerability, involving relationships which are sinister, and jobs become dependent on collusion, a situation we all have to deal with. The Catch-22 situation is the need to pay bills and keep the job while having to continually justify to ourselves that we are being personally unprincipled and behaving and going along with something abhorrent.

In the state of vulnerability, it is a personal matter of how to cope with it and which options to employ, including the following:

- full frontal confrontation,
- acceptance and capitulation,
- waiting for the opportune moment to deal with it,
- denying it to accept it and make the best of it.
- Whatever the reaction, the strategy to cope is factual.

The bigger picture

If vulnerability impinges from the outside, from the local environment, it has an omniscient quality and the individual becomes a team player. How to react becomes less obvious and becomes more democratic with the inherent danger of reducing the impact and diluting the responsibility.

Further, on the inside of a person is there a more sinister vulnerability – the vulnerability of lifestyle preventing actual brain development. We now know a bit more of how the brain is interconnected. However, in work with brain-damaged children and with the children discussed above in the case studies, I saw children diagnosed as retarded. What I needed to do was to facilitate development.

Fads, fashions, trends: Daring to be different

Fads, fashions, trends and following leaders, have been a survival strategy employed since civilisation began. Our ancestors would follow a leader to where the group could survive, where pastures provided food and water would quench their thirst. They would create pathways which made the journey from food to water easy and well-trodden. The group would provide protection from predators and reduce the risks for individuals living alone. Thus, the hierarchical system would lead individuals to want to aspire to the top of the hierarchy and emulate the successful members, adopting the same characteristics and acquiring the same weapons and wealth. These patterns can be seen to increase and maintain the competitive edge to fuel progress. Even the collie dog knows that he needs to keep the flock together if he is to herd the flock successfully into a safe enclosure.

The apostle Paul recognised and knew that the need of the successful evangelising of the early church depended on banding believers together and was key to the spreading of Christianity. Herding and banding together has played a foundational part in the success of hunter-gathers in the past up to the present day, and the model has spread to governance, politics, finance, etc.

In the same way, psychology has fuelled present-day trends in fashion, art, music, diets and adornments such as tattoos. These fads, which are transient, have followers, and marketing strategists use and exploit this need to follow, copy and eulogise.

However, the real progression has come from the solo players, those who have dared to be different, who have risked and given up the security generated by being full paid-up members of a group, those who have questioned the cogency of just following. They have seen the fragility of following trendy behaviour fads and fashions and have dared to look deeper and probe below the superficial to see the danger of throwing in their lot with the mainstream ideologies.

In science, we set hypotheses, which we test for significance through analysis and repeatability as we are looking for verification. But some will question the data. For example, people love graphs; they are seduced and mesmerised by the way graphs appear authentic and coherent with the lines demonstrating upward or downward trends. They are sold ideas and services, yet few will venture to ask, "How did you select your cohort? What criteria did you use?"

The danger in following trends, in whatever sphere of society, is that if the trend is dangerous, with consequences such as life or death, economic collapse or political upheaval, then in this day and age, when so many are involved, the consequences are proportional and can potentially be catastrophic. Take, for example, tattoos. When I had to write a report on HIV and Aids, tattooing was a concern because of the need to use needles which penetrated the skin with indelible ink. I had to visit these premises and report on the dangers. At the time, I felt that acquiring Aids by this means was a risk, purely because drug users did have tattoos as a mark of belonging to their culture. However, because of the pain, the risks and the fact that they were there for life, I never thought they would be a risk to the general public. How wrong I was! Now, the exception is the person who has not got a tattoo. Of course, the consequence and risks are not just associated with illness and infections: people who want to remove the tattoos claim they are causing them psychological distress and, therefore, the NHS should remove them. If, suddenly, tattoos were to become a mark of derision, rather than of belonging to a sub-culture, potentially, the surgical capacity of hospitals to remove them could undermine the real purpose of the NHS, which is to heal the sick.

My intervention with patients necessitated working to unravel the past and, in the present, to prepare for the future. To do this, they had to work at improving their physical health to access their mental functioning. I was trying to access their acumen, their thought processes, encouraging contemplation and aiming at wisdom. In this day and age, the mobile phone may be in danger of denying children the ability to think and develop in a rounded manner. Sadly, I witness children sitting in buggies while their mothers/carers are glued to their mobiles. Children are then offered the devices as a form of play. Is this safe or is this a sinister indication of turning away from providing the basics which children need to develop? And does this mean that what I advocate for patients to turn them round will become redundant (i.e. the simple message of listening to them and me being able to work with them)?

Chapter 19
Emotions Kill: Unpacking the Flip Side of Christmas, Weddings and Funerals

This chapter is concerned with the form and the content of family events. Celebrations, whether they be joyous such as marriage, Christmas or the celebration of life, are highly charged emotional events. But should we assume that with emotionally charged situations and events, there is the inevitability of factions? If so, what do we need to do to avoid them?

As a family therapist, I can't stop myself from observing and attempting to unpack family dynamics and trying to come to some understanding of separate events, at least to my own satisfaction. Recently, I've observed at close quarters the anguish caused by three events which should have been celebrations, but which turned out to be disconcerting to all those involved: Christmas, a funeral and a wedding. In each event, there was a polarisation which forced those intimately involved to take a side, be defensive, or take the middle ground by sitting uncomfortably on the proverbial fence. Those on the periphery and non-family members are probably blissfully unaware of the issues being fought out prior to the event.

The first event to unpack is Christmas. Christmas was historically the celebration of the birth of a baby born in a manger. Change in society around the year AD 336 caused the date of 25 December to become established as the day to celebrate Jesus's birth. The bearing of gifts most probably originated in the story of the three wise men bearing frankincense, incense and myrrh, symbolic gifts to the baby Jesus. The legend of Santa Claus can be traced back hundreds of years to a monk named St Nicholas. It is believed that Nicholas was born sometime around AD 280 in Patara, near Myra in modern-day Turkey. Much admired for his piety and kindness, St Nicholas became the subject of many legends. Now he is principally associated with the bearer of gifts to children at Christmas.

Christmas has now largely lost its religious meaning to worship and give thanks for the birth of Jesus, a gift to the world. It is estimated that only 10% of western populations centre Christmas around church-going. Christmas has become a more pagan festival for family get-togethers and extremes of indulgence.

Originally, these celebrations would have a short preparation time. For example, Charles Dickens portrays the Cratchit family as buying the turkey on the same morning as it was eaten. Nowadays, the countdown to Christmas usually begins in November – some six weeks before Christmas Day. Similarly, all these celebrations now have a much longer gestation period. Christmas marks the end of the year when summer has finally gone, and we are propelled into the realisation that we have to face six months of cold weather, darkness, dampness and snow, impelling us to alter course and prepare. Shops seduce customers to buy presents, decorations, food and drink and to begin preparations. Partying begins well before 25th December as office parties are booked well in advance to avoid disappointment due to competition. Christmas usually lasts for two days, but for some, even Boxing Day is given over to shopping and taking advantage of the sales. A lot of time, thought and money is invested in the preparation for these two days. People order furniture and shops set deadlines and promise to deliver 'in time for Christmas'. As the big day draws near, the atmosphere becomes charged to reach the day fully prepared and with great expectations. There is only so much food that can be eaten or drink that can be drunk, and recreational outlets, such as sports and hunting, take place as a healthy antidote to all the excesses on Boxing Day.

Some people spend more than they can reasonably afford, and only in the new year, when bank statements arrive, will the expenditure become a reality. Christmas-spending statistics show that 'tis the season to be spending. New research reveals that 36.3 million Brits plan to spend an estimated £14.2 billion this festive season'. Despite all the sometimes-painful memories of former years and mistakes made, often the expectations of all this time and money will fall short, and the New Year will begin with regrets and bills.

Not unsurprisingly, with such huge investment, Christmas is also a time when emotions come to the fore, lubricated by alcohol and unrealistic expectations. Every emotional arousal calls for pre-determined coping strategies to be employed to escape the aftermath and repercussions of hostilities and slights which result from these festivities. For the long-term good and for the cohesion and survival of families, compromises have to be made. However unpalatable, it may be necessary to join with in-laws and family members with whom we don't get on. Or we may just need to support all the endeavours made by those hosting the event and for the long-term good. Alcohol fuels both the pleasure and the shortcomings of Christmas. Some, according to their personalities, will find that their choices and resultant behaviour will spoil the celebrations and sabotage the event, with the outpouring of anger, prompted by jealousy, envy, etc.

Weddings

A wedding is the celebration of two people being legally bound in marriage, of entering into a contract. This too has biblical origins, but once again, these are largely bypassed. It is not unusual for the wedding to be planned years in advance, which gives the family time to save for the big day. The average wedding in the UK now costs £30,355, a new survey has revealed. According to bridebook.co.uk's National Wedding Survey (2018), the cost of getting married has hit an all-time high, up by £3,365, or 12%, from £26,989 the previous year.

While many family members may agree to put aside their differences on the wedding day, this isn't always the case. In many complicated family situations, emotions tend to peak around major family events – and the wedding is no exception. Family get-togethers are becoming fewer as people move around the globe. A consequence is that, on the few occasions when families do get together, old scores erupt, although few would consider a wedding the right time to settle scores or to sort out family feuds and sabotage the occasion.

Families could be estranged, and the untangling of relationships at a wedding is difficult. Divorce brings to the fore righteous indignation and the tangles which ensue. These tangles unfortunately need to be anticipated and managed at a wedding, sad as it may seem. Divorced parents may issue ultimatums such as "I'll only attend if that person isn't invited", or stipulate that they will attend only if their new spouse is invited. These selfish demands put pressure on the couple being married to focus on the demands of their families rather on the importance of the ceremony and the commitment they are making to each other – at a time when they should be surrounded by the love and support they need from their families to have a future together.

Funerals

Funerals are more sombre but, nevertheless, intended to celebrate a life, with the expectation by some that the person will inherit eternal life. The average cost of a funeral in the UK is £4,798 for a burial, with average cremation funeral costs at £3,744.

The relationships with the deceased will determine matters and decisions concerning whether to attend the funeral service and then deciding whether to go to the wake after the funeral. Break-ups, divorces and re-marriages will add complications regarding duty and genuine sadness. As they do for Christmas and weddings, family rifts again come to the fore. The rector of our church surprised me by saying that it is not unusual to have a police presence at a funeral when different factions between family members were anticipated. Concerns about inheritance and the unfair distribution of wealth inevitably starts at a funeral, having been contained during the lifetime of the departed.

Relationships and grudges surface during a funeral. The reasons and causes may appear meaningless in comparison with the death, but in some cases, the death ignites the hostilities, while in others, each party goes their separate ways never to meet again.

All family events

So, if these are the events, what do they have in common and why do they provoke such outbursts of emotions and repercussions which undermine the very purpose of organising them in the first place? The most obvious reasons are the following:

- alcohol disinhibition,
- highly charged emotions,
- long gestations,
- investment of time, thought and money,
- cessation, conclusions and departures.

Alcohol is the most commonly used mind-altering substance. The National Institute on Alcohol Abuse and Alcoholism (NIAAA) reports that over half of all American adults were current drinkers of alcohol at the time of the 2015 national survey. Having a beer or a glass of wine with dinner is common, and millions of adults regularly enjoy alcohol responsibly.

Alcohol is definitely part of celebrations even though alcohol is a depressant substance which acts on moods, emotions, actions and reactions. It is often used to get the party going. When people drink, they say and do things they would not normally do as they become disinhibited. The more alcohol the less inhibition and potentially, the less control over actions. "Alcohol changes brain chemistry, which in turn impacts moods, behaviours, thinking, memory, physical movement and bodily functions, which may have costly side effects."

Alcohol shrinks the brain, making memory, mental illness and learning worse over time. Symptoms coupled with reduced mobility are caused by thiamine deficiency, which may be triggered by drinking too much. Even moderate drinking, which is 1–2 servings of alcohol per day, may cause damage to cognition and memory. These are the health consequences, and as important as they are here, we are concerned with the undermining of personal and social relationships. Clearly, there is no dividing line between the two.

Just recently, the newspaper reported the death of a young man who, under the influence of wine, for a dare swallowed a slug, which happened to be crawling over the table. Months later, he was dead; the slug had caused an infection in his brain which killed him.

A few drinks make everyone more sociable and increase camaraderie, but they also increase the likelihood of drinking to excess, becoming aggressive and being unable to remember what happened the next day. Celebrations can end up as far-from-convivial occasions.

Conclusion

Briefly, we have unpacked the negativity of these events, and what we have seen is that underlying all the behaviour and content in all these celebrations are the emotions, which are defined as strong feelings deriving from one's circumstances, mood or relationships with others.

Emotions are unleashed in the lead up, during and in the aftermath of these specific occasions. Celebrations are undermined by the personalities and behaviour resulting from highly charged emotions which are often lubricated and released with the consumption of alcohol.

So, what is the answer? How should we deal with these emotions we don't want, and what are they? There is no denying that emotions are good and necessary, but we are focusing on the negative emotions that threaten to destroy celebrations intended to celebrate, emotions such as anger, jealousy, guilt, hostility and aggression. Every emotion has its own costs and benefits (Lazarus, 1994). 'The danger is that the feeble gains derived from aggression arising from anger, envy and jealousy will blind us to the far more damaging losses that are more often its harvest.' In my own work (Thomson, 2017), I relate that I was not surprised to see how prominent emotions were in the aetiology of mental illness and how often jealousy was pivotal.

So, what is the answer? Well, to start, it is knowing ourselves. It takes courage to unpeel the layers we have formed around us to protect us from the truth. Knowing our shortcomings and anticipating them involves planning ahead. We need to ask ourselves such questions as: In the past, have we suffered the consequences of being the life and soul of the party? Is it comfortable? What have the consequences been? Or have we become angry and said things so cataclysmic that the consequences are irreparable? We need to take decisions on whether to attend an event at all, how much to drink, who is best to go with and who can accompany us home.

These are soul-searching questions which can only be decided sitting down quietly alone. Emotions are obscure, but if they are recurring, it is worth examining them. Take anger, for example. If anger is an emotion experienced repeatedly, something has triggered that anger such as feeling vulnerable or being slighted, which can then lead to inappropriate acts. Envy is when you want what someone else has, whereas jealousy is when you're worried someone's trying to take what you have. Identifying patterns may be helpful in avoiding situations with the potential to trigger unwanted emotions. For example, if they occur after a few drinks, then the trigger is the release of inhibition by the alcohol and the solution is either don't drink or moderate your consumption. If they occur in certain company, then they can be avoided. So, what is the solution? Walk away.

This honesty is transferrable; it can then be used to understand others, who most likely suffer the same problem. They, in turn, will know exactly how to trigger negative behaviour in others, which then boosts their own egos. Emotions give control to our adversaries. But most importantly, gaining this insight places control where it should be – within ourselves. Emotions do kill – festivities, relationships, celebrations and, in some extreme circumstances, actual human beings!

Chapter 20
Conclusion

My hope is that by sharing my experience, so-called personality disorders will be considered differently and that services which are starting up, failing or just unable to ever discharge patients will reconsider strategies to bring about change. I've treated many patients, but these are the patients I most enjoyed, from that first encounter, through the journey, to the final farewell, which though sad, was wonderful and a privilege.

If there is one message in my journey which jumps off the page, it is the need for prevention. I was asked to be a member of a group of health professionals to work on a curriculum providing children with the education they needed to live successful, meaningful lives, equipping them with a toolbox of skills and wisdom which would alert them to dangers and potential problems. I was very pleased to be included in the group. As a therapist, I was dealing with young people who had fallen victim to the dangers within society. As I have shown, for everyone I saw, there are now thousands whose lives are tragically wasted and marked by suffering as typified by Jake, who realised he could never catch up.

I attended the group and suggested that from beginning school until reaching leaving age, children should have, as part of the school curriculum, lessons to prepare them for life, enabling them to be aware of right and wrong but also covering issues such as the law and how society works. The curriculum should include both the practical and the emotional, a knowledge of family dynamics and risk of infatuation. The curriculum would cover all the deficits and pitfalls that I, as a therapist, had discovered. I can remember being quite passionate about this initiative, only to learn that my recommendations had been discounted. The others, mostly educationists, saw no need for my advice.

This really upset me because I had always made it my business to investigate the schools the children were attending (if they were indeed at school). I enjoyed working with the schools; usually these relationships were educational (i.e. once they had dealt with one case, they then could apply that knowledge to another). They would be rewarded by a successful outcome. Sadly, there were a few instances when the teachers were sadistic, punishing children like William when they arrived at school late because a parent never cared enough to get them ready for school.

As I've said, these emotionally deprived, ill children look ill. Usually because they are neglected, they are physically compromised as well through not sleeping comfortably and not eating nourishing meals. When they wear the wrong clothes and look unkempt and out of place, their classmates bully and scapegoat them. But more specifically, these children wear a dull expression and have sunken hollow eyes, and it so obvious that something is wrong. To punish these children due to ignorance is a crime. All schools need to be vigilant, and just as they make provision for the gifted and talented children, there needs to be provision for schools to replace the shortfalls in family care.

The teachers need to look out for struggling children and to have case studies like those above discussed as part of their training – as do social workers, doctors and anyone working in the caring professions. What was very obvious to me was how patients remembered very clearly, down to the last detail, the events which hurt them. All the case histories are littered with these memories, such as Jake waiting in his bedroom while relatives he had never met were discussing his mother's death and his future with an abusive father and his sadistic wife; or Adele's photographs of her cousins which she cherished before her adoptive parents split up.

One of the items close to my heart for including in a school curriculum on prevention would be infatuation. I've alluded to the responsibility of society to be setting examples to children as they grow. The media, the obsession with mobile phones and instant communication is, in my mind, toxic. It is depriving children of exploring and developing naturally as sitting glued to a computer screen is unhealthy. Their brains are developing and they need to experience touching, making, running, climbing, being bored and solving boredom. We are in danger of producing a generation of children who are under-developed and under-achieving, who, when they become adults, will have the capacity to produce children but will be lacking the ability and experience to raise them. They will be quite unsuitable to become parents themselves and provide care for the next and subsequent generations. For example, some children, nowadays, are being sent to school at five, lacking toilet-training.

As a therapist, I defined infatuation as 'an intense but short-lived passion or admiration for someone or something', as in, 'he had developed an infatuation with the girl' and included 'a passion for, love for, adoration of, desire for, fondness for, feeling for, regard for, devotion to, penchant for, preoccupation with, obsession with, fixation with, craze for, mania for, addiction to'.

I was party to the lengths particularly girls would go to get their man – stooping to the greatest lengths, dressing provocatively, having sex, even becoming pregnant and trapping young men into making a long-term commitment, which resulted in relationships doomed to fail and producing children who became the victims. These situations need to be part of education; infatuation is a pitfall with huge social and emotional consequences.

Chapter 21
The Do's and Don'ts of Being a Professional and Treating Patients

Don't become a therapist if

- you can't cope with heartbreak – it's part of the territory and our job is to see beyond the hopeless;
- you haven't a sense of humour;
- you're not prepared to put patients first;
- you don't like a challenge;
- you are not a risk-taker;
- you need praise to sustain you;
- you are unsure of your own identity;
- you don't have a list of people whom you can tap for help.
  Do become a therapist if you have all the attributes in the list of don'ts and if
- you are wanting to achieve and do something worthwhile other than being a pop-star or a footballer;
- you are intuitive and interested;
- you are loving, giving and generous;
- you are resilient and can take failure on the chin, regroup and up sticks;
- you enjoy excitement and a challenge.

If in writing this book I have painted a picture which has left you unmoved, I have failed. If that picture appears hopeless, I have also failed. Dr Prewer, a psychiatrist I once knew, asked me what I wanted to be if I could have chosen another career. I said a sculptress. He said, "You have sculpted patients' minds. That is your calling."

I must admit the work is exciting, exhilarating and humorous. If you like a challenge, there is no greater reward than discharging a patient, knowing they are ready to take on the world. If they can overcome adversity and situations which appeared devastating, then that is a resource available to them which few will have available. On that note, I was once asked to apply for a job within social services, and I went to meet the director and several of her staff. She explained that the job involved spending time in court, preparing court reports, etc. I wasn't persuaded and I dared to say that I found my work exciting.

I took a group (of which Fergus was a member) who were chronic alcoholics, habitual drug takers, patients who were in a revolving roundabout situation, a cycle that involved offending, appearing in court and ending up prison or in hospital, etc. Everyone had given them up and there was absolutely no optimism, evidence or reason to believe that they would ever get off this roundabout. They had somehow gravitated to me and the group kept growing. Looking back, I find it intriguing how this whole thing came about. But now, recalling the members of the group, I wish that I could go back and pick up where I left off. It was so successful.

I want to make a last attempt to reinforce the main aim of this book which is to emphasise the need to develop a bottom-up approach attuned to the needs of the patients. This initiative began because I was headhunted to leave the drop-in centre and become a manager in a psychiatric hospital. I was required to give three months' notice, but the hospital wanted me to give only a month's notice and to begin work urgently. My departure from the drop-in centre would leave a vacuum, so I was asked to take my patients with me. Those patients enjoyed the facilities of the hospital. My new office was, in fact, a flat previously occupied by doctors. This flat had a lounge, a kitchen, a bedroom and bathroom – facilities! So, naturally, I exploited them.

Being a hospital, there was always a need for extra hands, so to receive a midday meal, the patients could clock in at nine for coffee and biscuits, have a chat and then do jobs around the hospital. The wards began to ask for their help with various jobs, and the patients would enjoy being useful. Then, as I could see the need to give the patients something back, I needed funding.

So, the administrative staff would bring in cakes for sale, and staff would pop in for coffee. This was good for the patients to meet people whom they would not encounter in their daily lives. It was also good for the admin staff, who were only connected to patients via writing letters for the consultants, otherwise, they never met the patients. Then the patients turned their hands to washing cars, for which they were paid, so my slush fund was growing. I could afford to pay for an artist, a drama teacher and a craft lady.

Now, just to gain some insight and perspective, previously, these patients had two alternatives: to commit suicide or to kill themselves slowly by taking drugs or drinking themselves to death and thereby face a hopeless future. In other words, getting on and off that roundabout. But because for them life at the hospital by comparison with their past was so much better, they never bemoaned their situations. They brought a zeal, a humour and genuine concern for each other into the group. As you have read, Fergus laughed when he told the story of the rats eating his shoes while he was sleeping on a tombstone in the cemetery! They would laugh about the need to store empty bottles by placing them in the sleeves of coats, or about their fear that the garage roof might collapse because he hid empty bottles there. It was often hilarious and very exhilarating in comparison with stereotyped services.

Naturally, I needed friends to run what was a service without funding. The administrative staff would make cakes, help with posters or provide paper for the art class. The caterer would provide meals which the patients had in the flat and for which I didn't pay. The receptionist issued bus passes which were so crucial at weekends when the group didn't meet. I conclude with this because looking back, what my intervention lacked was continuing support. So often, these chronic patients have no one. This group provided each other with a surrogate family which they had never had.

Bibliography

Ackner, B (1954). Depersonalization I: Aetiology and phenomenology. *Journal of Mental Science, 100*, 838–853.

The Association for Family Therapy. (1999). Oxford: Blackwell.

Barrett, P T, & Kline, P (1980). Personality factors in the Eysenck Personality Questionnaire. *Personality and Individual Differences, 1*, 317–333.

Berkman, L F, & Syme, S L (1979). Social networks, host resistance and mortality: A nine year follow up study of Alameda County residents. *American Journal of Epidemiology, 109*, 186–204.

Bishop L F, & Reichart, P (1971). Emotions and heart failure. *Psychosomatics, 12*, 412–415.

Booth, T J, & Cottone, R R (2000). Measurements, classification and prediction of paradigm adherence of marriage and family therapists. *The American Journal of Family Therapy, 28*(4), 329–346.

Bridebook.co.uk's National Wedding Survey (2018)

Burton, N (date). *The Meaning of Madness.*

Cattell, R B (1965). *Scientific study of personality*. London: Penguin.

Cassel, J (1976). The contribution of social environment to host resistance. *American Journal of Epidemiology, 104*(2), 107–123.

Cronbach, (1990). *Essentials of psychological testing.* New York: Harper Collins.

Durkheim, E *Suicide: A study in sociology.* The Free Press

Emotion; Definition of emotion in English by Oxford Dictionaries

Eysenck, H J (1967). *The biological basis of personality.* Springfield, IL: Thomas.

Eysenck, H J, & Eysenck, S B G (1975). *Manual of the Eysenck Personality Questionnaire*. London: Hodder and Stoughton.

Glezer R, Felthous, A R, Holzer, C E (2002). *Animal cruelty and psychiatric disorders. Journal of American Acada Psychiatry Law*, *30*, 257–65.

Grossarth, R M, & Eysenck, H J (1990). Personality, stress, disease: Description and validation of a new inventory. *Psychological Reports*, *66*, 355–373.

Hopes, L M, & Williams, A (1999). Depression, self-defeating, and self-destructive behaviours as predictors of suicide ideation in males and females. *Psychological Reports, 84*, 63–66.

Hinkle, L, & Wolff, H G (1957). The nature of man's adaptation to his total environment and the relation of this to illness. *Arch's Intern. Med.*, *99*, 442.

https://www.history.com/topics/christmas/santa-claus

Joreskog, K G (1993). Testing structural equation models. In K A Bollen & J S Long (Eds.), *Testing structural equation models* (need page range). New York: Sage Publications.

Jung, K (1998). *The essential Jung*. Fontana

Kelley, K, Byrne, D, Przybyla, D P J, Eberly, C, Eberly, B, Greendlinger, V, Wan, C K, & Gorsky, J (2005). Chronic self-destructiveness: Conceptualization, measurement and initial validation of the construct. *Motivation and Emotion*, *9*, 135–151.

Kelly, D B, Rollings, A L, & Harmon, J G (2005). Chronic self-destructiveness, hopelessness and risk-taking in college students. *Psychological Reports*, *96*, 620–524.

Kessler, R, McLaughlin, K, Green, J, Gruber, M, Sampson, N, Zaslavsky, A, Williams, D (2010). Childhood adversities and adult psychopathology in the WHO World Mental Health Surveys. *British Journal of Psychiatry, 197*(5), 378–385. doi:10.1192/bjp.bp.110.080499.

Kline, P, & Barrett, P T (1983). The factors in personality questionnaires. *Advances in Behaviour Research and Therapy*, *5*, 141–202.

Lazarus, R S, & Lazarus, B N (1994). *Passion and reason: Making sense of our emotions*. Oxford University Press.

Lebow, J (2005). *Handbook of clinical family therapy*. Hoboken, NJ: John Wile.

Lewin, R (1992). *Complexity: Life at the edge of chaos.* New York: Macmillan.

Model Selection for Identifying Power-Law Scaling https://research.vu.nl/ws/portalfiles/portal/42161240/chapter+3.pdf

National Institute on Alcohol Abuse and Alcoholism.

Nunally, J, & Bernstein, I (1994). *Psychometric theory.* New York: McGraw-Hill.

Pagels, H (2008). *The dreams of reason: The computer and the rise of the sciences of complexity.*

Querido, A (1959). Forecast and follow-up. *Brit. J Preventative Soc. Med., 13,* 33

Rutter, M (1999). Resilience concepts and findings: Implications for family therapy. *The Journal of Family Therapy, 21,* 119–144.

Selye, H (1974). *Stress without distress.* Hodder & Stoughton.

Spielberger, C (1972). *Anxiety: Current trends in theory and research.* New York, NY: Academic Press.

Sun Life's 2018 Cost of Dying Report. (2018).

Thomson (nee Evans), W (1980). Stress and psychoticism. *Personality & Individual Differences, 2,* 21–24.

Thomson (nee Evans), W (1986). Personality and stress. *Personality & Individual Differences, 7*(2), 251–253.

Thomson, W (1996). Type of depression and results of mortality. *Personality and Individual Differences, 21*(4), 613–615.

Thomson, W (2011). Lifting the shroud on depression. *Journal of Affective Disorders, 130,* 60–65.

Thomson, W (2012). Long-term follow-ups of suicide in a clinically depressed community sample. *Journal of Affective Disorders, 139*(1), 52–55.
https://doi.org/10.1016/j.jad.2012.02.012.

Thomson, W (2014a). *Depression, neuroticism and the discrepancy between actual and ideal self-perception.*

Thomson, W (2014b). The head stands accused by the heart! Depression and premature death from ischaemic heart disease. *Open Journal of Depression,* 3(2), 33–40.
https://file.scirp.org/Html/1-2720024_45352.html.

Thomson, W (2014c). Rate of stroke death following depression: A 40-year longitudinal study extension of Chichester/Salisbury Catchment Area Study. *Journal of Stroke & Cerebrovascular Diseases*, *23*(7), 1837–1842. https://doi.org/10.1016/j.jstrokecerebrovasdis.2014.03.013.

Thomson, W (2016b). Depression, neuroticism and the discrepancy between actual and ideal self-perception. *Personality & Individual Differences*, *88*, 219–224. https://doi.org/10.1016/j.paid.2015.09.003.

Thomson, W (2017c). Sabotaging the self: A trait and its relationship with neuroticism. *Clinical and Experimental Psychology*, *3*(4), 175.

https://doi.org/10.4172/2471-2701.1000175.